THE ROAD TO ABA

*a study of british administrative policy
in eastern nigeria*

THE ROAD
TO ABA

*a study of british administrative policy
in eastern nigeria*

HARRY A. GAILEY

london   UNIVERSITY OF LONDON PRESS LTD
new york   NEW YORK UNIVERSITY PRESS

JQ 3099
E 23 G35

105351
ISBN 0 340 11594 7

Published by University of London Press Ltd 1971
First published in the U.S.A. by New York University Press 1970
Copyright © 1970 New York University

University of London Press Ltd
St. Paul's House, Warwick Lane, London EC4P 4AH

Printed in Great Britain by Lewis Reprints Limited,
Port Talbot, Glamorgan.

77-11519

Preface

This book reflects my continuing interest in the mechanisms of control utilized in the twentieth century by the British in governing their African territories. The presumption which I followed in a previous work, investigating the administration of the Gambia, underlies also the choice of Eastern Nigeria as the focal point of this study. Stresses occasioned by European imperialism in an African society can be examined most clearly when the political system imposed by the imperial power does not conform to the traditional political form. In this respect the Ibo and Ibibio areas are even better subjects for analysis than the Gambia since the local government devised for them was almost completely at variance with their village-based polities.

I am primarily concerned in this work with three subject areas. These are the establishment of British rule, the imposition of a type of local government on the people, and finally the people's rejection of this system. The focus of the study is on the British administration in Eastern Nigeria and its attempts to rule a vast, nearly incomprehensible area. Secondary to this

interest is a concern with the Ibo and Ibibio and their acquies-
cence in the synthetic system devised by the British. How did
their compliance change their society and why and how did a
particular segment oppose a continuation of the system of
"warrant chiefs"? Had conditions in Eastern Nigeria been different in the spring of 1967, I might have gone more deeply
into the Women's Riots, utilizing interviews with old men and
women in the villages. However, it was not possible to pursue
these ambitions and I was forced to rely to a great extent on
official publications for this section. Another point should be
made concerning the opening chapters. In the chapter describing
the people of the East, I have tried to give only a brief outline
of the very complex Ibo and Ibibio society. To have attempted
more would have meant shifting the focus of the book. In the
chapter dealing with early European contacts I have merely
sketched the background so that later more detailed examina-
tions of British policy would have continuity. Professors G. I.
Jones, K. Onwuka Dike, and J. C. Anene have already done an
admirable job in closely examining the Eastern areas in the
nineteenth century.

This work was made possible by a grant from the Social
Science Research Council which enabled me to investigate the
Nigerian archives. I wish to thank all persons involved for my
selection and support, but particularly Mr. Rowland Mitchell.
In Nigeria my gratitude must first go to Dr. Robert Armstrong
who, as head of the African Institute at the University of
Ibadan, made available to me all the services of his office and
who also had the patience to listen as I talked out certain problems. I wish to thank Professor S. M. (Tekana) Tamuno
of Ibadan and Professor A. E. Afigbo of Nsukka for allowing
me access to their unpublished theses. Professors J. F. Ade Ajayi
and J. C. Anene also took time from their busy schedules to help
me. The assistance of Dr. Richard Mastain, formerly of the
Peace Corps, was invaluable to me in my wanderings in Eastern Nigeria. No expression of appreciation would be complete
without mention of the Chief Archivist and his first-rate staff
at Ibadan as well as the staff of the University Library. In
England the personnel of the Colonial Office Library and the

British Museum were as usual most helpful. The Public Record Office continues to amaze me with its organization and efficiency, and I wish to add the staff of the Round Room to the list of people who helped me.

I hope that to a modest extent I have done justice to an ⸳interesting and important topic and thus in part repaid the selfless help I have received from scores of people.

Harry A. Gailey
Los Gatos, California

Glossary

One must be clear concerning the British use of certain terms related to local government in Nigeria. The following definitions, therefore, should be used as a guide to understand the development of courts and government through the first three decades of the twentieth century.

A *Native Court* was a court designed by the British authorities and was composed primarily of African members. These could be "minor" courts or "Native Councils" as referred to by the Ordinances of 1900 and 1901 or designated A, B, C, D as in the legislation of 1914. A Native Court had jurisdiction over a number of villages in a given area. Minor courts had areas smaller than major grade assigned to them. Some major Native Courts acted as appelate courts in judicial matters for inferior courts within a given territory. Until the mid-1930s the Warrant Chiefs who presided over many Native Courts had not only judicial, but also legislative and executive authority. The basic administrative unit for Eastern Nigeria from 1914 to 1929 was the Native Court Area.

Native Authority as used by Lord Lugard referred to a

unit of local government which would exercise executive, legislative, and financial control over a specific area. Its functions would be separate from those of the courts. A Native Authority could be defined as an individual or a series of individuals elected or appointed, and recognized by the British government as possessing such authority. During the 1920s the Warrant Chiefs were normally defined as Native Authorities, although experts such as Sir Donald Cameron later disputed such a definition. Cameron used the terms *Native Authority* and *Native Administration* interchangeably to denote an agency which was given certain executive and legislative authority.

Traditional Authority designated that system of social and political control which was operative before the British conquered Nigeria. Thus the term applies to such highly structured systems as the Muslim Emirates of the North or the Yoruba states of the West and also the loosely conceived, village-based, nonchiefly systems of the Ibo and Ibibio. One factor which most of the systems had in common was the blending of executive, legislative, and judicial authority together in one man or a single agency.

Native Treasury both as envisioned by Lugard and later carried into effect in the latter 1930s was an important subdivision of a Native Authority. It was supposed to be staffed by Africans and was to prepare a local budget, collect taxes, disburse funds, and maintain good records of such transactions. Although British district officers were, ideally, to be relieved of the bulk of such financial responsibilities, they remained throughout the 1940s the chief financial officers of most Native Authorities.

Contents

Preface   v

Glossary   ix

Introduction   1

I. The Land and the People   9

II. The Growth of British Influence   31

III. The Establishment of British Control   51

IV. The Decision to Tax   75

V. The Beginning of the Disturbances   97

VI. The Spread of the Revolt   115

VII. The Government's Reaction   135

Appendix
    A. Biographies of Major British
       Administrators   157
    B. Bibliography   163

Notes   169

Index   179

THE ROAD TO ABA

*a study of british administrative policy
in eastern nigeria*

Introduction

Most of the territories which would later constitute
Britain's dependent empire in Africa were acquired reluctantly
in the two decades after 1880. The dominant imperial attitudes
of British leaders of both major parties in the mid-Victorian
period were vehemently opposed to the acquisition of territory.
A large influential segment of British government opinion recommended the casting off of colonies such as Canada, New
South Wales, New Zealand, Victoria, and Cape Colony. This
did not imply an anti-imperial attitude as some later observers
seemed to believe. Rather it reflected the successful business-
man's view of empire. Britain, dominant in manufacturing, trade,
and finance, did not need colonies or dependent territories to
assure its prosperity and continued growth. The most important
areas for British trade during this high period of free trade
were not her colonies but independent states in Europe and
North and South America. Briefly stated, all British governments prior to 1880 were concerned with increasing British
profits. It was believed that colonies added nothing to the economic posture of Britain. On the contrary, their administration

cost money and, as in the case of Canada, some were constant sources of friction between Britain and other foreign governments.

These antiexpansionist attitudes had a great effect upon the administrative structure designed to rule the empire. The Colonial Office was viewed by most politicians as a second-class ministry. Therefore, the most influential and competent men in both parties demanded other portfolios. Not until Joseph Chamberlain chose the Colonial Office in 1895 was there a politician of the first rank in charge of Colonial affairs. The staff of the Colonial Office was always very small for the task of governing such a large and diverse empire. Inevitably, due to the work load, certain priorities were established—in fact if not in theory. Decisions related to the larger, more important colonies had first call upon staff time. African affairs were seldom considered in the same category as those of the major colonies. The bulk of decision making was done by clerks who read incoming dispatches and wrote minute papers recommending solutions to problems raised by overseas officials. Normally the Permanent Undersecretary and the Colonial Secretary accepted a clerk's minute with little or no modification. The few British possessions in Africa prior to the "scramble" were administered from London by persons who knew little about the territory being governed. The Colonial Office was primarily concerned with keeping in check administrators whose zeal might outrun the policy of nonexpansion.

The fifteen-year period before 1895 was a transition period from economic to territorial imperialism. Pressed by the expansion of other European powers, the British Government reluctantly abandoned its older concepts. In Nigeria, French and German activities were the incentive for the establishment of a British Protectorate over the Oil Rivers in 1885 and over the Lagos hinterland in 1893. Further in the interior, Sir George Goldie's Royal Niger Company was empowered by the Crown in 1887 not only to trade, but to rule over territories ceded to it or placed under its protection. Continuing French activity in Dahomey and the Western Sudan showed that Goldie's company was not the proper vehicle for assuring British hegemony over disputed territory.

After 1895 the British Government was openly committed to the acquisition of territory. It was unwilling to share with its competitors any African territory that it claimed. The most obvious examples of this new policy are the Sudan and South Africa. However, one can also note its effect in Nigeria. Areas such as Benin which had not been greatly affected by the British presence were brought under control. The Protectorate over the Lagos interior was made functionally operative by active administrators backed by troops. The Royal Niger Company police were replaced by an imperial force and by the turn of the century the Crown had assumed direct responsibility for governing the company's territories. The forward policies of Sir Frederick Lugard in the North and Sir Ralph Moor in the East were approved and supported by the Home government.

During the transition phase and, later, the period of active territorial imperialism, no fundamental changes were made in the system of governing dependent territories. Colony areas immediately adjacent to Lagos, Freetown, Bathurst, and the Gold Coast strip were not appreciably increased in size. The governors of these colonies were simply made responsible for the newly acquired protectorates. During the period of expansion it appears that the Colonial Office did not have a clear, all-embracing definition of a protectorate. A territory was simply declared to be such as a device to assure British supremacy. The legal ramifications of the declaration were worked out after occupation. One factor of primary importance to the future of these protectorates was the dominant role played by the Exchequer in overseas expansion and development. The policy that it had followed during the so-called "little England" period was carried over into the more activist era. Government officials after 1895 were given more staff and provided with more military force. Seldom were the forces, however, of the requisite size to assure the commander's success if an African kingdom chose to fight instead of negotiate. As soon as a pro-

B

tectorate had been established, the Treasury demanded the paring down of costs of administration to as low a level as possible. It was, as one observer remarked, getting an empire on the cheap.

Lack of adequate troops and sufficient funds meant that British administrators in the field had to compromise with African leaders. This was particularly the case when they were confronted with such powerful potential opponents as the Fulani emirates in the north. The extension of crown-colony government, which was essentially autocratic, obviously would not work in an undiluted form in the new protectorates. Some hybrid had to be devised to allow ultimate control to rest with the British while reserving to the native administrative systems most of the details of government. Drawing partially upon their experience of ruling India and partially upon the necessity to compromise with African polities, the British instituted systems of protectorate government which have come to be called "indirect rule."

However varied its actual provisions in separate territories, indirect rule was a magnificent compromise between direct British control and independence for the African. Very early in each protectorate there was established a skeleton staff of British administrative officers whose locus of authority was the Governor of the Colony. The major function of the protectorate staff was to maintain order in its district and to see that the provisions of ordinances and proclamations issued by the Governor and his associates were observed by local authorities. This *de facto* system functioned best wherever there existed an efficient African bureaucracy such as in the northern emirates. After the initial period of conquest or occupation had passed it was therefore logical to look to these areas for guidelines in order to make indirect rule work equally well in other territories. In Nigeria the organized Muslim North exercised a dominant influence over the planning for and execution of native administration elsewhere.

Indirect rule, that magnificent pragmatic system to which a generation of British administrators and theoreticians would later give philosophical and moral buttressing, did not, in retrospect, work well in any African territory. However sincere the purpose, the practice everywhere shifted real authority away from traditional leaders to the British administrative superstructure. Indirect rule at its inception was a method by which a few administrators could rule a vast territory with a minuscule amount of money. The rapidity of the occupation of Africa and the small size of the Colonial Office staff, at home and in the field, made it impossible to become familiar with traditional systems of rule. There were repeated instances in which the British chose the wrong man for a responsible position, and in all areas of British jurisdiction there existed the game of chief making. Despite criticisms, indirect rule worked best wherever there was a well-ordered African bureaucracy. This is not to imply that those traditional rulers supported by the British carried on traditional rule. It was simply to the advantage of the chiefs and the people to accept the "indirect" form of government since it did preserve intact some of their laws and practices, and retained for the chiefs the right of low-level decision making.

There were a few areas in Africa where from the beginning the system which the British thought traditional was so at variance with actuality that it could be maintained only by force or the threat of force. Such an area was southeastern Nigeria. Conquered rapidly in the opening years of the twentieth century, the village-oriented Ibo and Ibibio peoples were immediately presented with a political form that had no counterpart in their experience. Forced immediately to create a governmental organization, the British did not have the time or the talent to understand the incredibly complex social and political structures of these Eastern people. Their assumptions took two forms. One was that the Ibo and Ibibio had once had a system of chiefs which had simply broken down or decayed under the impact of slave trading. The other, equally wrong, was that the hinterland Ibo and Ibibio represented a much lower level of development than other West African people. In either case, the British reasoned, the native-authority system that they were introducing was a distinct improvement over the previous village-based polities.

Gradually the British imposed a political structure on the Ibo and Ibibio, the keystone of which was a native-court area with a chief who had received from the British a warrant to rule. Seldom were these new chiefs drawn from the traditional village leaders; the British usually used these positions to reward Africans who had helped them during the period of occupation. Nor were the villagers blameless in the selection of the new rulers. Few villages, confronted with the frightful potential of the British, wished to expose their elderly leaders to unknown dangers—so they simply refused to identify their influential men. The "warrant chiefs," completely alien to the traditional systems, became increasingly dependent upon the British district and provincial officers. The warrant chiefs and their principal aides, the Native Court clerks, dominated the Native Courts as well as having executive authority. In both capacities many chiefs were incompetent and corrupt. Under such conditions it was not surprising that village elders continued, in the twenty years after pacification, to make the major decisions affecting their villages. British administrators made many ineffectual attempts to curb the influence of the traditional village leaders and to bolster the esteem of the warrant chiefs. By the mid-1920's the tensions between the theoretical and actual local governments of the Eastern territories had reached the point where major changes in the system were recommended by almost every district officer in the area.

The decentralized nature of their societies had made it difficult for the Ibo and Ibibio to oppose the initial British conquest. Later it made any concerted opposition to the foreign mode of government nearly impossible. Even on the village level men were cowed, remembering the strength and marveling at the wisdom of the white men. After more than twenty-five years of misrule, the Governor of Nigeria, ignoring the advice of most of his district officers, decided to force the Eastern areas to conform to government practices prevalent elsewhere throughout Nigeria. To accomplish this, district officers were ordered to make detailed surveys of all the native-court areas. This collection of data was made not to understand the traditional systems of authority, but in order to tax the

Eastern areas. The central Government, not satisfied with the imposition of a tax upon people who had never been taxed, decided upon a complex system mainly because it was the type used elsewhere in Nigeria. The violence feared by many district officers did not materialize and the first year's taxes were collected from the seemingly docile villagers. The pent-up resentment and frustration of the Ibo and Ibibio, however, burst out in the following year after rumors that women were going to be taxed.

The Ibo and Ibibio women, believing in a special type of immunity and utilizing their secret societies and the markets to spread the revolt, tried to bring down the synthetic, British-created system of chiefs. In December 1929, the women failed in their immediate objective, but they did force the British Government to investigate carefully indirect rule in Eastern Nigeria. Then for the first time, despite the many previous ordinances and proclamations, officials at all levels tried to understand the complex social and political systems of the Ibo and Ibibio. With the possibility that all of Eastern Nigeria might soon be in revolt against them, the British finally discovered that the entire basis of their rule was questionable. The Colonial Office then began to investigate the Northern-oriented, tidy administrative method created by Lord Lugard and his successors. The new Governor, Sir Donald Cameron, within a short time scrapped the old scheme and issued new Native Authority Ordinances. The changes in local government instituted between 1930 and the beginning of World War II did not give back to the people traditional rule. This had in many cases been upset, undermined, or destroyed by the previous warrant-chief system. What did emerge was a reasonable compromise between traditional and modern colonial forms of administration. The history of Eastern Nigeria after 1930 is testimony to Cameron's wisdom in sponsoring decentralized local-government agencies.

CHAPTER I

The Land and the People

The disturbances in Eastern Nigeria in December 1929 had their roots in the complex interplay between British idealism, pragmatism, and ignorance. The realities of European competition had demanded a rapid conquest of the Eastern hinterland. Once conquered, the areas had to be governed with a minimum of expense. Idealism dictated that the new political structures be as close as possible to traditional forms while preventing certain activities believed to be repugnant to humanity. The third factor, British ignorance of the hinterland peoples, effectively foiled the ends of idealism. By their conquests, the British had assumed responsibility over peoples who had perhaps the most complex social and political structures in Africa. It is necessary, therefore, before attempting an examination of the course of British policy in Eastern Nigeria which culminated in the Women's Riots, to examine the physical environment and in a general way explain the most important aspects of the native societies of the East.

The geography of Eastern Nigeria is dominated by one salient feature, the Niger River.[1] The coastal region westward from the city of Bonny is a maze of major and minor outlets of the great river. The fourteen-thousand-square-mile delta is so complex that Europeans who had traded along the coast for four hundred years had not suspected that it was the outlet for the mystery river of West Africa until 1831 when it was confirmed that the Niger River, rising in the Futa Jallon, was fragmented near its outlet. It was later discovered that the most important branches of the Niger were the Benin, Forcados, Nun, New Calabar, Brass, and Bonny rivers. Further to the east there are the Imo, Kwa Ibo, and Cross Rivers which have their sources in the highlands of Eastern Nigeria and the Cameroon.

The land rises gradually from the Bight of Biafra to a sloping, low-lying region, overgrown with mangrove swamps that are cut through by numerous rivers and creeks. The bulk of this mangrove and fresh-water swampy region is located in southeastern Owerri Province. Southern Calabar Province has only about eight hundred square miles of coastal mangrove. There are two other more important zones in Calabar Province. One is the cultivated riverine lands, particularly those on either side of the Cross River. The western riverine lands of the Cross begin only ten miles north of the ocean and extend all the way to the northern boundary of the province. The other zone is the high rain forest which covers approximately three thousand square miles. In many parts of this belt today there has been considerable clearing of the forest.

From the low-lying swampy areas of the delta, the land in Owerri Province rises northeastward to a gently inclined tableland which covers the central portion of the province. From the borders of this area the land rises more sharply to the northern hill country of Onitsha and Ogoja provinces. Owerri Province, as well as southeastern Benin and Warri provinces, is covered by either high forest or secondary growth. The secondary forest would soon revert to high forest if not continually cleared and cultivated. Ogoja and Onitsha provinces are mainly grassland and savanna.

The soils of Calabar and Owerri provinces are generally light and sandy except in the northeastern section of the latter where mixed clay and loams are found. Fertility throughout most of the area varies from moderate to poor. The bulk of the inland population is engaged in subsistence farming with the major emphasis upon growing yams. These are planted in mounds each year in March or April. The crop is harvested once without disturbing the vines so that a second growth of tubers will yield supplies for the next planting. Cassava is also a major crop, largely because it grows well in poor soils and needs little care. Ibo and Ibibio farmers also grow some maize, peppers, beans, and cocoa yams.[2]

The oil palm provides the major money crops for Eastern farmers. It grows wild in the secondary forest and around settlements but not in the high forest or savanna. Oil palms provide both oil and kernels for export. Trees producing the best, or soft, oil are found in the Ibibio areas of Calabar Province, extending northward into Aba Division of Owerri Province. The hard-oil territory covers Warri and most of Owerri Province.[3]

A large portion of the secondary forest in Ahoada, Aba, Owerri, and Bende divisions of Owerri Province is generally underfarmed, as is the relatively fertile savanna land north of Enugu. These areas also have low population densities, rarely exceeding one hundred and fifty per square mile. The bulk of Aba and Bende divisions of Owerri Province, Calabar Division of Calabar Province, and the Afikpo Division is heavily cultivated with many yam farms and extensive palm groves. The approximate population density in these divisions is three hundred per square mile. Much of the land in the Agatu, Orlu, and Udoko divisions of Onitsha Province, and in southern Okigwi and northern Owerri provinces, is overfarmed. Most of the trees with the exception of oil palms have been eliminated. Population pressure is greatest here with densities varying between four hundred and eight hundred per square mile.[4]

The physical environment of Eastern Nigeria, by comparison with other West African territories, is quite favorable, but it has imposed certain distinct limits upon the people. The complex river system, even after coastal trade became important, served to isolate one group from another. The high forest acted in the same fashion, making communication difficult even between villages inhabited by the same peoples. Defense against invaders, particularly before the general use of firearms, was much easier than in the open savannas. Change—political, social, or for that matter linguistic—could be resisted. It was extremely difficult for any group to impose a centralized political scheme upon the scattered Ibo and Ibibio who had never developed a system of chiefs before moving into the forested areas. Without traditions of unitary or bureaucratic government, members of the same people living for a few generations in the forest environment began to grow apart. This is one of the main factors accounting for the multiplicity of Ibo and Ibibio linguistic, social, and political forms.

In any brief survey of the peoples of Eastern Nigeria it is logical to begin with the coastal groups. The major people of the central and eastern delta are the Ijaw.[5] Before the arrival of Europeans, the Ijaw lived in small villages of a few hundred inhabitants situated along the creeks of the delta. The most important of these villages were Brass, Okikra, New Calabar, and Bonny. The Ijaw engaged in some agriculture and trade, but the major economic pursuit in pre-slave-trading days was fishing. The political system was also village oriented and normally very similar in organization to Ibibio villages. A number of patrilineal, extended families made up a ward and several wards combined to form the village. Ward heads were usually chosen on the basis of age with economic power a secondary criterion. The titular head of the village was called the *Amanyanabo* and was normally chosen from only one of the lineage groups in the village. His role aside from presiding over the village assembly was, in pre-European days, largely ritualistic.[6]

The arrival of European slave traders worked profound changes on the Ijaw towns. The thinly populated areas in their immediate hinterland could not supply the demand for slaves and it became necessary to enter into closer trade relations with the more heavily populated Ibo areas. The advent of firearms enabled some of the towns enjoying favorable locations to monopolize the slave trade over a very large area. Many of the Ijaw towns grew rapidly in size due to this concentration of power and the importation of large numbers of slaves. The new factor of great profits introduced more indivdualism to the societies. Increasingly, economic achievement became the measure of success rather than an inherited position. Although previously the amanyanabos had performed a basically ceremonial function, they began to assume real political power. In conjunction with leading traders, they now made decisions binding on all the people.

By the eighteenth century in all the coastal towns the old ward organization had given way to the institution of the house —or more accurately, the canoe house. The head of a house was a wealthy trader who in effect became a chief. All of the chief's lineal descendants and slaves were members of the house and the powers of a head over these members were considerable. He had the right of disposal of all property including the wives and slaves of petty chiefs. His judicial powers extended sometimes even to the settlement of homicide cases. Disputes between houses were usually referred to a general assembly of the town and sometimes the Aro oracle of the *Long Juju* became the final arbiter.[7]

The political influence of a house ultimately depended upon its economic position. Each house maintained a war canoe manned by as many as fifty men and sometimes armed with cannon. In addition to this naval force, the house owned a large number of trading canoes which brought from the interior the human goods on which the prosperity of the house depended. A house might also own a part of a major town, several smaller towns, and parcels of land scattered throughout the area. The head of a house encouraged members to set up their own trading ventures since this increased the political power of the house in the assembly as well as increasing its wealth. In order to keep this expensive operation functioning, the head assessed trading members up to 25 per cent of their profits.[8]

It should be noted that the same forces that compelled changes in the Ijaw political structure operated among the Ibibio coastal towns. With certain modifications, the king-house system typical of the Ijaw towns was also present in the Ibibio areas, of which Old Calabar was the most important.[9] European traders and later political representatives encouraged the continuation of the centralized political and economic structures in the coastal towns. However, they believed that the institution of chiefs and houses was traditional and not a recent innovation largely caused by the slave trade.

The Ibibio were an imporant coastal people who, in the 19th century lived in the area between the Imo and Cross Rivers. In contrast to the Ijaw, however, the Ibibio also occupied a large portion of the hinterland as far north as the Aro country. The relatively new institutions of the house and the chief systems affected only a small portion of the Ibibio lands immediately adjacent to the coast. In the interior, although the slave trade had an economic impact, it did not seriously affect the decentralized village mode of government.

Anthropologists, using largely linguistic factors, in the 20th century have divided the Ibibio into six major segments. The name Ibibio originally referred only to the largest group which is sometimes also called the Eastern. However, the term by extension is now used to denote all of the related people. In addition to the Ibibio subdivision, the five other groups are the Western or Anang, the Northern or Enyong, the Southern or Eket, the Delta or Andoni-Ibeno, and the riverine or Efik.

The Eastern Ibibio, or Ibibio proper, are at present located in the largest numbers north of the Delta Ibibio in Uyo, Itu, Ikot-Ekpene, and Opobo Divisions of Calabar Province.[10] The soils throughout this area are sandy clay and were, even in the 1920's, much impoverished, particularly in Uyo Division. Most of the Ibibio were dependent, therefore, upon palm products. From the raffia palm they got the materials for baskets, palm wine, and illicit gin. The oil palm provided kernels and oil which enabled Ibibio villagers to live and prosper on poor land despite high population densities.

The Western or Anang today inhabit an area from just north of Ikot-Ekpene to Abak in the south and from the Imo River eastward almost to the Kwa Ibo River. They seem to have originated from a single group located near the present town of Abak and were the last people in Calabar Province to come into contact with Europeans. The population density of Anang areas in the 20th century has been very high and the farmland was not enough to support the population. Fortunately there were large numbers of oil and raffia palm trees in the area and this has modified the effects of overpopulation.[11]

The Delta or Andoni-Ibeno at the time of the British occupation were a very small group which occupied thirty-two islands and mudflats extending inland approximately ten miles from the coast between the Bonny and Cross Rivers.[12] There is some question whether, because of their language and matrilineal organization, they should be considered Ibibio. Some experts consider them to be descendants of the original Ibibio stock who escaped to the creeks and swamps and preserved their social organization from later patrilineal invaders. The Andoni did little farming and did not harvest or market palm products. Their society earned its livelihood from fishing and the sale of smoked fish.

The Southern or Eket peoples seem to have migrated northward from the Ibeno areas to their present location in Eket Division of Calabar Province.[13] Their chief source of income was from farming cassava, yam, and cocoa yam, but they also engaged in some fishing. The Oron tribe of the Eket were noted for their carving of ancestral figures and the women also constructed decorated calabashes and mats. The village and the village cluster (the *afaha*) were the most important traditional political divisions.

The tiny Northern or Enyong group is located east of Bende to the Cross River.[14] They differed more from the generalized linguistic, social, and political pattern than any other Ibibio group except the Andoni.

The final subdivision of the Ibibio is the Efik.[15] They were probably the last of the Ibibio to move to their present location along the eastern bank and near the mouth of the Cross River. The ancestors of the Efik were very likely Eastern Ibibio who migrated southward and founded fishing villages along the river and creeks. The most important of these were Creek Town and Old Calabar. Because of their favorable trading location, the Efik were most influenced by the slave trade. The transformation of traditional social and political organization which affected the Ijaw villages also took place among the Efik. The house system became firmly established, particularly at Calabar, although the heads of houses, *Etuboms*, never exercised as much authority over the members as did their counterparts among the Ijaw. Another major difference was that even though trading became very important, the Efik never lost touch with the land.

From this melange of present day differing groups one can abtstract certain common features in Ibibio social and political organization which probably are unchanged from the time of the British occupation earlier in this century. If this is true, then the basis of society was the nuclear family composed of a man, his wives, and children. The lowest level of effective political organization was the extended family, a unit of several nuclear families. In most Ibibio areas an extended family occupied part or all of a continuous compound. A cluster of such households made up a ward under the secular control of an elder (*Ete Otung*). In some cases this secular leader was not the head of the patrilineage (*Ete Ekpuk*). In such an eventuality the ward head would not reach a major decision without the prior consent of the Ete Ekpuk. Male members of the patrilineage formed the nucleus of the ward, having collective rights to the land. A combination of several wards constituted a village. It was in Ibibio villages, as in their Ibo counterparts, that most important political decisions were made. The village head (*Ete Idung*) was chosen from the ward lineage heads. The village head was not an autocrat since his power was limited by the rights of heads of families and ward leaders. Decisions affecting the village were normally arrived at by a consensus of these leaders. Religious beliefs and religious leaders also helped block one-man rule, even on the village level.[16]

A further important check on usurpation of power was the presence of age sets. These served the main function of education for both sexes from the age of ten until after marriage. However, they remained active until the members had reached middle age. Age sets were considered guardians of public morality and had the right of punishing their members for bad behavior. The sets could also act as policemen and in some cases were given the power of imposing fines.[17]

Even more important than age sets in providing leadership

not dependent upon an official political position were the title societies. There were four different societies for men and one major one for women among the Ibibio. The men's societies were the Ekpo, the Idiong, the Ekong, and the Ekpe. Only the latter was not of Ibibio origin, having been developed by the Ikoi people east of the Cross River. There were significant differences in the philosophical basis and ritual forms of each society, but they all performed similar necessary functions for the village. The societies had the responsibility of protecting the community from harm through magical and religious means. This usually meant driving out bad spirits that could harm the community. Each society exercised rigid control over its members and by extension over the entire community. Membership in all the societies depended upon kinship and the possession of some wealth, since to move from the lower grades of a society, advanced titles had to be purchased. The leader of the secret society was not necessarily the village head although the latter would be a member of the society. In those areas where the society was considered to have jurisdiction, the village head became a servant of the society.

The women's society called Ebre, also village based, was open to all adult women. The society had authority over all unmarried girls and all ceremonies relating to girls and women. It defined the proper conduct for women and had the power to punish violations of the code. It also planned and carried out the various dances and celebrations in which women took part, particularly at the time of harvest.[18]

The place women have held in Ibibio society is difficult to assess. In many ways their status seems to have been no higher than in more centralized, authoritarian systems, particularly in the matter of marriages and divorces. The girl's family, in consultation with that of the prospective bridegroom, was responsible for the betrothal. In obtaining a divorce the husband had more latitude than the woman since he did not have to prove justification. In cases of divorce the children of the marriage usually remained with the father to whose lineage they belonged. Despite their apparently subservient role, Ibibio women did enjoy considerable freedom and power. They belonged to their own societies and these had real power in deciding issues relating to women. Then, too, although responsible for a great share of the work of harvesting, women could claim certain products as their own. Surplus food products could be traded at markets for profit. The women became major traders, particularly after the introduction of European products. The necessity of traveling to and from markets and the possession of the money earned gave adult women a freedom and economic power unusual among African people.

Above the Ibibio village there were theoretically three higher political levels. The first was the village group or town which was composed of several villages. One village was normally recognized as senior and thus would provide an elder who served as the religious leader of the town. The town would also have a secular leader who presided over a council of elders to arrive at decisions affecting all villages. Despite such an organization, the bulk of decision making was on the village level. Most of the actions taken by town leaders related to religion and kinship links. In times of crisis, elders of different towns in a given locale could meet together to decide upon common strategy. There was no formal political machinery established for this village group. An even more amorphous entity among the Ibibio was the subtribe composed of people with a common name, institutions, and dialect. The subtribe was something to which the inhabitants of different villages recognized they belonged but which traditionally had no effective political organization. In later government reports, the subtribe was renamed the clan and given a type of status which in practice it had never possessed.[19]

In recapitulation one can say that the traditional Ibibio political system was decentralized. Any unity within a subtribe was that of common religious beliefs and social practices. To the extent that a villager met proper citizenship requirements, he was expected to and did participate directly in decision making, usually on the village level. The presence within a village of different organizations, each charged with executive and moral functions, effectively prevented undue concentration of power. The policies of the trading cities along the coast in restricting

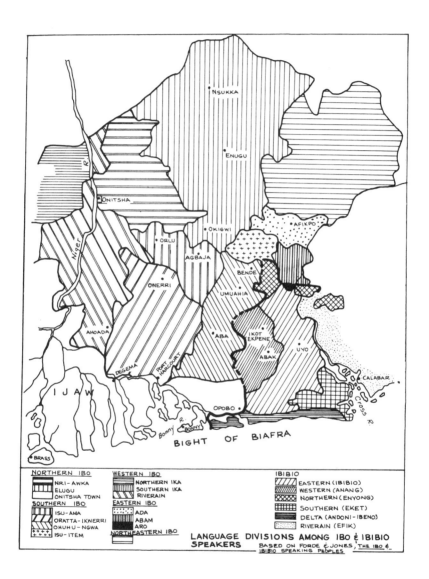

LANGUAGE DIVISIONS AMONG IBO & IBIBIO SPEAKERS

BASED ON FORDE & JONES, THE IBO & IBIBIO SPEAKING PEOPLES

NORTHERN IBO
- NRI-AWKA
- ELUGU
- ONITSHA TOWN

SOUTHERN IBO
- ISU-AMA
- ORATTA-IKWERRI
- OKUHU-NGWA
- ISU-ITEM

WESTERN IBO
- NORTHERN IKA
- SOUTHERN IKA
- RIVERAIN

EASTERN IBO
- ADA
- ABAM
- ARO

NORTHEASTERN IBO

IBIBIO
- EASTERN (IBIBIO)
- WESTERN (ANANG)
- NORTHERN (ENYONG)
- SOUTHERN (EKET)
- DELTA (ANDONI-IBENO)
- RIVERAIN (EFIK)

C

Europeans from moving freely into their spheres of influence cushioned most Ibibio villages from rapid economic and political change. Only among the Ibibio in the vicinity of Old Calabar were there radical alterations in the decentralized form of government.

Adjacent to Ibibio territory to the north and west live the Ibo, the most numerous and today the most important people of Eastern Nigeria. They occupy an area of approximately fifteen thousand square miles, including the entirety of Onitsha Province, all of Owerri Province with the exception of small areas of Bende and Ahoada Division, almost all of Afikpo and Abakaliki divisions of Ogoja Province, and about 50 per cent of Aro Chukwu District of Calabar Province. There are also considerable Ibo settlements west of the Niger River in Benin and Warri provinces.

Despite the vast areas occupied by the Ibo, they were protected from European contact until late in the nineteenth century. Thus there was no long interlude between the first contacts and the military occupation of their country—and the British conquerors knew even less of the Ibo than they did of the Ibibio. The difficulty of the Ibo languages and the complexity of their society, combined with the preconceptions of the British administrators, resulted in a continuing ignorance of the Ibo on the part of the invaders. Only after 1927 was there recognition by more than a few district officers that Ibo society was among the most complex in Africa and that it should be thoroughly studied. The riots of December 1929 underscored this need for the British to investigate the Ibo in order to reform the native administrations. The majority of the intelligence reports compiled in the early 1930's in response to the riots were done by overworked district officers who had little anthropological training. In the years preceding Nigerian independence, when Ibo society was changing rapidly, a few excellent anthropological and linguistic studies were made. However, the fact remains that even today there are many unanswered questions about the Ibo, and until further field work is done many of the generalizations concerning them will be speculative.

Even the use of the term *Ibo* (more accurately *Igbo*) poses certain questions. One author, himself an Ibo, states that originally the term *ndi igbo* meant only men of the hinterland as contrasted to the people who lived along the Niger River and its branches who were called *ndi olu*. The riverine people used *igbo* as a term of contempt for lesser peoples. However, the hinterland peoples, because of their superiority in numbers, in time gave their name to radically differing kinds of societies.[20] Traders, and later British officials, continued to use the term *Ibo* as if it referred to one people. But in reality the British were not dealing with "a single homogeneous people but with a collection of heterogeneous peoples who were united by a name that is neither apt for nor acceptable to some of them and bound together—uneasily—by a language, the dialects of which are often no more like each other than Italian is like Spanish." [21]

Ibo languages belong to the Kwa group of African languages. There are two major spoken dialects, Owerri and Onitsha Ibo. These terms are somewhat confusing since the dialects are not restricted just to these provinces. Owerri Ibo is spoken more extensively than any other dialect. Furthermore, among the northern Ibo there are two major dialect clusters, that of the Nri-Awka group and that of the Enugwu group. In addition, the people of Onitsha town speak a variant of Nri-Awka and this form has been adopted by many people in the surrounding areas. There are wide differences in construction, vocabulary, and phonetic structure among all the dialects. Some linguists have noted that there is as much difference between extremes of the Ibo language as between modern English and the language of the Saxon invaders of England. To further confuse the linguistic pattern, Protestant missionaries, confronted with such a multiplicity of Ibo dialects, constructed their own written form. Called Union Ibo, it was used to produce Ibo Bibles and to serve as a literary language for use in schools. Union Ibo, however, was not very successful in displacing any of the older dialects.[22]

Other terms such as *tribe*, *subtribe*, and *clan* also cause difficulty because they describe social and political subdivisions which did not exist among the Ibo before the imposition of

British rule. Administrators, particularly after the investigations preceding taxation, gave a political reality and power to the clan which had no precedent in native society. Thus it became the cornerstone of the reconstructed native administration in the 1930's. There were in reality, prior to that time, only four viable political divisions among the Ibo. These were the extended family, the *umunna* or localized patrilineage, the village, and the town or group of villages.

The family household, although not in itself a political unit, was the foundation on which all more complex Ibo institutions were based. It consisted of a man, his wives, and other dependents. It included married sons whatever their age, but not married daughters. Marriage among the Ibo was everywhere patrilocal and potentially polygamous. There was no polyandry anywhere in Iboland. As long as the head of the family lived he was the spiritual leader, had the final voice in land distribution, and represented the family in any litigation with outsiders. Descent among the Ibo was patrilineal except in certain societies near Afikpo which followed a form of matriarchy. At the death of the head, the group could choose to break up and divide the land or to stay together. In the latter case the eldest son of the deceased or his eldest son became the new head.[23]

The lowest political division with real meaning among the Ibo was the extended family and it was composed normally of twenty or more family households. The extended family traditionally lived together in a walled-in area. It had its own political leader (an *okpala*), title holders, and age grades. However, political decisions at this level were generally very democratic. They were taken only after the widest consultation, both formal and informal. Women's opinions were important and their leaders were consulted in private. If the decision was very important, the women would hold their own formal meetings to reach a consensus.[24]

The extended family was a part of a localized patrilineage (*umunna*). It should be noted that Ibo used the term umunna, *i.e.*, children of the same father, in an imprecise fashion to describe a number of different things. Used to describe a localized patrilineage, it referred to all descendants of a particular ancestor who occupied the same territory or village. Wives were counted as a part of the umunna but married daughters were not. The umunna was exogamous. In some areas of Iboland sexual relationship between members was taboo and to break the rule was a crime against society.

The patrilineage was known by the name of a semi-mythical ancestor. The head of this subdivision of several hundred persons was called the okpala or in some areas the *opara* or *diokpa*. He was the eldest living male of the senior branch of the mythical family. The okpala had religious and social as well as political functions to perform and his power depended upon his knowledge, wisdom, and strength. Traditionally he worked in conjunction with a council of elders. In some places, however, real political power rested with a number of prosperous men who had gone through certain ceremonies and ·expended a considerable sum to acquire a title. Where the title societies were this important, the okpala might not even be a part of the decision-making body unless he had taken a title.[25]

The village, composed of a number of umunna, was the strongest social and political unit among the Ibo. Villages varied in area from one-half square mile to upward of six square miles and in population from a few hundred persons to over two thousand. The village was based upon common kinship, religion, language, and economic ties. Each village recognized one umunna as senior, based upon descent from the founder. The eldest man of this branch held the senior staff of office (*ofo*). He bore the same title, okpala or diokpa, as the head of a umunna although he had much greater authority and power than these lesser officials. The actual power wielded by the okpala of the village depended largely upon his personality. If a strong man, he ran the village in fact as well as in theory, with the council and titleholders supporting his policies. If weak, he became a figurehead and real decision making was done by other agencies.[26]

The largest political unit in Iboland was the association called by some scholars the town and by others the village-group. This was not just a collection of contiguous houses as in Western society. Composed of a number of villages, its size varied from less than four square miles to over thirty. The number of persons who belonged to a town could vary from a few hundred to tens of thousands. The political unit of a town was based on a number of factors. There was an identity or near identity of dialect spoken by all members. It was a mystical kinship unit where a common ancestor, usually of divine origin, was believed to have founded the town. His sons were considered the founders of the different villages that composed the town. Finally there was a central deity recognized by all members of the town. With the exception of the Western Ibo who had borrowed a more centralized form from Benin, the task of governing towns was relatively standardized. The senior ofo holder was a man who represented the eldest son of the founder of the town. His was an honorable but largely ceremonial position. Throughout most of Iboland the important decisions from the town were made by either a council of elders (*ndi ichie*) or a council of titleholders. In some towns governing power was in the hands of a ruling age grade which had been selected by the elders to have authority for a specified number of years.[27]

After the Aro Expedition in 1902 and the establishment of British regional government, the Ibo town lost much of its political significance. It ceased to be economically independent after the construction of roads and railroads. Nevertheless, the town still exercised a hold on people's loyalty. M. M. Green noted the direction and intensity of loyalties when she wrote in the 1930's:

> As with most peoples, in fact, the Ibo feel the bonds between them most closely when they are confronted by foreigners. Two men from whatever part of Ibo-speaking country when they meet in Lagos or in London will call themselves brothers. . . . At home, however, people will count themselves as belonging to their village-group, will feel themselves intimately members of their village, will recognize the neighbouring village-groups as people with whom they trade and will say of people beyond a radius of about seven miles: "The people of that place are very wicked." [28]

All observers agree that the village was the centrum of social, political, and economic life for the Ibo. There is also general agreement concerning the social structure of Ibo villages. In a traditional village there were three distinct divisions of society. These were the free citizens (*diala*), the slaves (*ohu*), and the religious slaves (*osu*). The free men through their patrilineage controlled the land and could participate freely in the religious and political life of the village. Through the process of consensus, no matter what their role, they had some voice in policy making. They all belonged to age sets, and if they were affluent they could purchase titles such as that of ozo. Although the actual power of title-holders varied greatly from one place to another, men who held a title were universally respected. Free women also belonged to age sets and their own societies, and because of tradition and their economic power were consulted on most important village matters.[29]

In addition to secret societies for both men and women, there existed in Iboland a voluntary grouping within villages called a *mikiri*. A mikiri could either be reserved for men or for women or be mixed. In the early twentieth century the organization served many functions. It was a social club, a debating society, and a savings bank. Meetings of the mikiri were held regularly, usually at least once a month. Each member was required to bring either one or two pence and some food to another member's house. The hostess would benefit by getting the money in return for providing service. Meetings were held on a rotating basis. Such groups as this provided women with easy contact with the affairs of men and allowed them to make their feelings known to village leaders without undue interferences in matters considered to be men's prerogatives.[30]

Slavery seems to have been an established fact in Ibo life even before the European slave trade became important for hinterland peoples. Slaves could be acquired by purchase or by kidnapping and were used mainly to labor on their owners' farms and compounds. Slaves, however, could be used as sacrifices to the gods, were often killed on the death of the master, and could be substituted for the owner if he had been convicted of a crime punishable by death. In some cases slaves were given land to farm and many acquired considerable wealth. Nevertheless, they could not marry free persons of the village nor take part in any of its political deliberations. There were still slaves among the Ibo, in fact as late as the 1930's, although they were not held legally. In a legal sense they were indentured servants who had pledged themselves to someone in return for money. They could redeem themselves from this position by paying off the original debt. Although no thorough studies are available, it appears that the social and political restrictions against such "servants" were still operative.[31]

The third class in Ibo society were the osu or religious slaves. Originally the osu or their ancestors were free. They were purchased by a family or individual on the advice of a diviner and were offered as the servant of some deity whose anger would not be placated by the usual sacrifices. From that moment the osu and all his descendants became members of a class apart. It was a crime against the village and the deity for any freeborn person to have sexual relations with an osu. They were regarded by the free with a sense of revulsion which was more basic than just a reaction to physical unattractiveness. Green reported that she had been told by an educated Ibo that in the old days an osu would be sacrificed instead of merely being considered a person apart. Therefore, members of the free society looked upon him as already being dead.[32]

The basis of economic life in all Ibo villages was subsistence agriculture, although a few more wealthy men owned some cattle, sheep, or goats. Therefore, many of the duties of the political leaders, particularly in their judicial capacities, related to land. The villages, except for some small areas dedicated to deities, did not own land. Ownership was typically divided among small groups of near-related kinsmen, branches of kindred, or the whole kindred. In most Ibo areas the pressure of population on the land was so great that all of it belonged to some landowning group. Women had certain land-use rights in the villages of their husbands but they could not own land. In some cases affluent women leased land. Rights of ownership were qualified because the land could be pledged or leased. It could not, however, be sold. The village, through the elders, supervised the dividing of land among heirs.[33]

In village life there was a division of agricultural labor between the men and women. A man was above all else a yam farmer. He was responsible for clearing the bush at the beginning of the season, and for making the mounds and planting the yams in February. When the tendrils of the yams began to grow he cut stakes and trained the vines around them. His work was then over for about four months until the first harvest, the time of cutting of the new yams. In some marginal areas there was only one harvest. In most areas, however, the second harvest was not completed until the end of October. Women were expected to feed their households. Although they sometimes helped with weeding and clearing the yam fields, they were concerned primarily with garden vegetables such as cocoa yam, beans, peppers, and okra. A woman was considered to own these. Any surplus over what it took to feed the family was hers to dispose of at the market.[34]

Trading was the second most important occupation of the Ibo. Markets were held every day of the Ibo four-day week in some village within a relatively short distance of any given village. In some places with a high population density, the number of days in the week was doubled to avoid conflicts between villages. Women were the main traders in the markets since they controlled much of the agricultural surplus. The larger markets normally began at noon while the smaller ones started later in the afternoon. Women with products to sell often left their villages before daybreak, returning home late in the evening. Profits were usually small although a few women became very wealthy trading in tobacco and spirits as well as foodstuffs. Some even traded in palm oil for which the profits were much higher.[35]

Markets also served functions totally unconnected with economics. They were a unifying force over very large areas since women from many villages met regularly at one place. Here they exchanged news and gossip which could be carried back to individual villages. Thus in a very short time news of an important event could be spread over most of Iboland. This explains why women located hundreds of miles away quickly knew the details of the beginnings of the Women's Riots at Oloko in December 1929.

Early in the twentieth century the collecting and preparation of oil products assumed new proportions for the Ibo. This was a task for both men and women. The men cut and helped carry the fruit while the women had the key roles in the very hard task of preparing the oil. The oil belonged to the man while the kernels were women's property. Oil production increasingly became the major way of obtaining money for the Ibo. Any fall in the price of palm products or the imposition of new duties affected an entire village.[36]

No survey of Ibo society would be complete without some reference to the Aro and their unique position among the Ibo in the nineteenth century.[37] The Aro homeland was centered on the site of the oracle or Long Juju at Aro-Chukwu. The Aros were a composite of three peoples—Ibo, Ibibio, and the Akpa who were of Okoyong origin. Tradition places the Ibibio first on the land. Presumably in the eighteenth century, Ibo invaders from the north entered the area. Neither people could overcome the other until the arrival of the Akpa from the south. The Akpa were probably armed with guns obtained by trade with the Europeans. By allying themselves with the new arrivals, the Ibo drove most of the Ibibio southward. The Akpas demanded and received from the Ibo a large portion of the conquered territory and settled on it. Scattered elements of the Ibibio also were allowed to collect near what is now one of the larger Aro towns, Obinkita.

The welding of these disparate elements into a formidable confederation is ascribed to Oke Nache, founder of the Aro royal house. Unlike most of the Ibo, Aro political organization was based upon the clan. Each village within the clan had the machinery to deal with its own affairs, with more important decisions reserved for a clan council. The head of the royal house, the *Eze Aro*, provided the necessary link between the various clans.

In this confederation the Ibibio supplied the concept of

the shrine, *Ibritam*, located by a small stream near the town of Ibom. The Ibo contributed the political organization and, more important, the ideas for the exploitation of the shrine. Under their leadership it became the most influential oracle in all of Nigeria and the fame of the Long Juju even spread far beyond the boundaries of Iboland. The Akpa, augmented by other warlike allies such as the Abam, supplied the military force for the confederation.

The Aro were not agriculturists but traders. They depended almost entirely on adjacent areas to supply their food. The special position of the Long Juju among the Ibo in the nineteenth century rather than military power made the Aro dominant in the hinterland. It is hardly conceivable that such a small number of persons could hold the numerically superior Ibo in subjection. Even in the 1920's the estimated population of the nineteen Aro towns was only nine thousand people. However, by clever utilization of the Long Juju, the Aro gained a virtual monopoly as middlemen between the up-country natives and the coast. Southern Nigeria east of the Niger was divided by the Aro into "spheres of influence." Each Aro town had its sphere and the right of building settlements and sending agents to that area. These settlements acted as clearing houses for trade goods and slaves. The shrine not only allowed the Aro to dominate the numerically superior Ibo, but was in itself a great producer of wealth. Fees and fines drawn from devotees brought in a tremendous income. It was estimated in 1912 that a greatly weakened Long Juju brought in £16,000 per year.[38]

The complex and almost inexplicable relationship between the Aro and the Ibo was completely misunderstood by the British. They believed that the Aro Confederation was primarily military and by the use of this power exercised autocratic control over subject peoples. This, combined with their general lack of knowledge of the Ibibio and Ibo, led them to believe that only by crushing the Aro in what was expected to be a hard, bloody campaign, would the hinterland be pacified. The speed and relative ease of the British takeover surprised the higher authorities. However, by pursuing their advantage, the British military columns quickly brought the bulk of Iboland under control. This type of conquest left no time to discover even the nominal Ibo political leaders, and certainly the early British administrators were almost totally ignorant of the complex system underpinning the "traditional" leaders. The need for some type of permanent local government system, nevertheless, had to be met. Sir Ralph Moor and his deputies provided one, and with a few minor modifications and one major overhaul by Sir Frederick Lugard, the theoretical structure, so at variance with reality, stood until December 1929.

CHAPTER II

The Growth of British Influence

European contact with the coastal people of Eastern Nigeria dates from the fifteenth century. At first concerned with exploring new territory and trading for tropical products, the Portuguese and later other European traders soon turned to the more lucrative trade in slaves. A large portion of all slaves collected by Europeans in Nigeria was procured from the eastern coastal region. The preoccupation of traders in the seventeenth and eighteenth centuries with human cargo which could be obtained relatively easily precluded any great interest in the interior regions. Trading companies and individual slavers were concerned with profits obtained at a minimal risk. European rulers, even at the height of their experiments in colonization, never seriously considered colonizing the unhealthy, inhospitable West Coast of Africa. They were concerned, if at all, with the maintenance of trade and the protection of their share from other continental powers. At the conclusion in 1763 of the series of wars between France and Britain—the so-called "Second Hundred Years' War"—Britain emerged as the greatest imperial power. Although the Nigerian slave trade was not

31

completely controlled by British merchants in the eighteenth century, their interests were dominant.

Some of the small Ijaw and Efik villages which occupied the more favorable locations along the coast developed into important trading states to answer the demand for slaves. They grew in size from villages of five hundred to one thousand persons to towns of over ten thousand people.[1] The structure of society at Bonny, New Calabar, Okikra, Brass, and Old Calabar was changed by the new opportunities offered by the slave trade. Chiefs who had previously acted as heads of councils now became hereditary monarchs and the chief traders of their towns. Access to European firearms accelerated this process, Economic success became more of a measure of importance than strict descent, particularly in the Ijaw towns. Slaves were important not only for export but also to provide the bulk of the labor force for the new towns. Treatment of slaves varied considerably from place to place. New Calabar and Bonny permitted slaves with real merit to rise to high positions in the state. Old Calabar, however, better insulated from competition, did not admit of such mobility and there was real oppression of the slave workers.[2]

In the eighteenth century there developed in the delta towns the institution of the house, or more exactly the canoe house. This consisted of a wealthy trader, his children, and slaves. The house maintained war and trading canoes. The head of a house, who was chosen by all the freeborn members on the death of his predecessor, had great powers over those persons who belonged to the house. Among the most important of these was the power to tax other members who engaged in trade. The establishment of the house system further concentrated economic and political power along the coast in the hands of a few wealthy men.[3]

The seemingly insatiable demands of the European traders for slaves could not be met by the coastal areas alone. The major towns depended upon the hinterland for a continuing supply. As already noted, this trade in Ibo territory was largely controlled by the Aro. The Aro maintained an efficient economic and religious organization and controlled the greatest oracle in Iboland. They maintained a complex trading network and their agents, particularly in the nineteenth century, were represented in all the regions of Iboland.[4]

Each of the major Ijaw towns was in direct trading competition with its neighbors and this led to a series of wars. Despite this, by the beginning of the nineteenth century there was established in the Eastern areas a real division of power and authority between the coastal traders and those who controlled the hinterland. It was to the advantage of both, but particularly to the coastal middlemen, to restrict the movement of Europeans into the hinterland. The native slave dealers of the towns realized that any direct contact with European traders by the suppliers of slaves would soon lead to their being by-passed and the rapid decline of their prosperity. Hostile attitudes by the coastal merchants toward white traders venturing into the interior, combined with the unhealthy climate, prevented the Europeans from acquiring knowledge of the interior much above the level of rumor.[5] How successful the coastal middlemen were in their efforts to deter the white traders can be seen by the speculations in Britain in the eighteenth century on the existence, course, and outlet of the Niger River, despite the thousands of Europeans who had traded in the delta for almost three centuries.

Three factors combined in the nineteenth century to end the trading stranglehold of the coastal towns over the interior. The first of these was an outgrowth of scientific curiosity in Britain and the desires of a few men to fill in the blank spaces on the map of the world. A series of expeditions beginning with that of Mungo Park in 1795 had by 1840 provided geographers and traders with basic knowledge of the rivers, land forms, and peoples of West Africa. Specifically for Nigeria, the explorations of Clapperton and of Richard and John Lander traced the course of the Niger to the sea, and their reports supported the merchants in their desire to open direct trade relations with the interior.

The abolition of the slave trade by Britain in 1807 was the second event which eventually ended the trading monopolies of the coastal towns. In order to enforce the decree on British subjects, the greatly strengthened West African Naval Squadron patrolled the Nigerian coast. The reversal of British attitudes had surprised the delta rulers since British traders had previously taken the largest number of slaves from the coast. The coastal traders, nevertheless, were happy to supply the needs of other European merchants of which the Spanish and Portuguese were the most important. Agreements between Britain, Spain, and Portugal in 1817 allowed the British to search suspected slavers of those countries. In 1836, the Equipment Treaty allowed the seizure of Portuguese and Spanish ships which had on board the machinery necessary for a slave voyage. The new activities of the naval patrol against these slave carriers was a severe blow to the delta towns.[6]

In the third place, the British Government brought direct pressure upon native traders to end their slaving activities. In some cases Britain secured treaties with the rulers whereby they promised to forego the slave trade. Needless to say the native rulers abrogated such treaties whenever possible. The presence in West African waters of so many British men-of-war led to armed clashes with the African slave traders. Bonny, which exported the largest number of slaves of all the delta towns, was a particular target for the antislavery patrol. By directly interfering in the politics of the town, Britain by the mid-1840's had forced many merchants to turn to legitimate trade. This had already occurred in most of the other major towns.[7]

Fortunately for the prosperity of the delta, there was no long delay between the decline of the slave trade and the discovery or cultivation of alternate products. The presence in the immediate hinterland of the oil palm and the growing demand for all types of oil in Europe meant that in the period 1807–1850 the delta towns could maintain their prosperity with only minor changes in their trading structure. In 1808, only two hundred tons of palm oil were exported from the Eastern regions. By 1845, oil exports had increased to twenty-five thousand tons.[8] Calabar was the first of the major towns to change from the slave to the oil trade. By midcentury, although trade in slaves continued, most of the towns were concerned primarily with the export of oil, and Bonny had become the chief port.

Liverpool provided the bulk of capital and men to exploit the oil trade. The so-called "palm-oil ruffians," however unsavory their image, firmly established a near monopoly by Britain over the coastal trade from the River areas to Lagos. They were prevented from penetrating into the interior regions as were their earlier counterparts, the slavers. The European supercargoes or agents were constrained to live in the coastal towns and barter for the oil with the heads of houses who controlled this rich trade as effectively as they had previously dominated the slave trade.[9]

Legitimate trade drew an increasing number of Europeans to the coast. In 1852, the British Government subsidized MacGregor Laird to operate a small fleet of steamships on the mail run to West Africa. Many men who could not previously have afforded the capital outlay now came to the delta. The new men soon discovered that they could undercut the older Liverpool merchants and use the steamships for the transport of their oil. This produced many conflicts in the trading community and also in the native towns. By the mid-1850's there were over two hundred trading firms operating along the coast.[10] The mechanics of the new trade and the large numbers of Europeans involved in it drew the British Government, against its will, into more direct intervention in the affairs of native communities.

John Beecroft, who had been involved with West Africa since 1827, was appointed British Consul to the Bights of Benin and Biafra in 1849. In the six years he held this office, he utilized his knowledge of the coastal peoples to further British trade and protect the traders.[11] This was dramatically illustrated by his interference in the affairs of Bonny and Old Calabar. Beecroft and the missionaries combined to influence the British Government in 1851 to overthrow King Kosoko in Lagos and establish the presumably more pliable Akitoye in his place. Continued intervention in internal affairs characterized the actions of the British consuls who succeeded Beecroft. The destruction of Old Calabar in 1855, king-making attempts in

D

Bonny, and the annexation of Lagos in 1861 are major evidences of government involvement in African domestic affairs in the consular period.[12]

Nigerian trade patterns were also upset by the activities of MacGregor Laird and Dr. William Baikie on the Niger River. Baikie's 1854 expedition proved conclusively that with proper precautions Europeans could live in the interior,[13] and in 1857 Laird received a Government subsidy to maintain steamer service on the Niger. Although his first steamer trading expedition was a failure, later ones, in conjunction with the missionaries, were successful in establishing trading posts at Aboh, Onitsha, and Lokoja.[14] Thus by using the Niger and steam, Laird and his associates flanked the Liverpool merchants and the African coastal middlemen who were forced to combine to counter the newcomers' threat to their trading position. Laird's steamers were bombarded with rifle and cannon fire and many were stopped and boarded by interior tribes friendly to the coastal traders. After 1861, Laird's ships were escorted up the Niger by naval vessels.

Baikie, from Lokoja, pioneered new trade connections with the north. He was instrumental in establishing friendly relations with the King of Nupe and in opening a direct trade route with Lagos. These efforts, combined with increasing British trade and missionary activity in Yorubaland, created pressures within the British Government, which demanded the opening of all interior areas of Nigeria to British traders. Despite the negative findings of the Select Committee of 1865, the Government was impelled first to interfere in the affairs of Yorubaland and then later in the civil strife of the midwest and delta areas.

Notwithstanding conflicts of goals and at times methods, merchants who wished to by-pass the African coastal middlemen by penetrating the interior found powerful allies in the missionaries.[15] Missionaries were imbued not only with the desire to convert the heathen and educate them to Western ways, but also to open new routes of trade. Missionary hostility toward traders was mainly because of the traders' permissive attitude toward repugnant native customs and the personal morality of

many of the European merchants. Merchants in their long association with Africans had changed the native societies only
on the periphery—with respect to some material desires. The
missionaries, on the contrary, aimed at changing the fundamental structure of native society by persuading the people to
embrace a completely new world outlook. To be sure, they
aimed first at abolishing such practices as human sacrifice, the
killing of twins, and the power of secret societies. Many missionaries, however, did not know that when large numbers accepted Christianity the entire fabric of the native society was
weakened. Christianity upset the delicate balance between politics, religion, and economics, and was as important as trade in
the latter part of the nineteenth century in inducing the British
Government to adopt a more interventionist policy in West
Africa.

The earliest effective missionary activity in Nigeria occurred in the West. By 1842, large numbers of Christian freed
slaves had been resettled at Badagry and Abeokuta. An important mission was founded in 1846 by the Church Missionary
Society at Abeokuta despite much local opposition. Five years
later missionary activities were extended to Lagos and in 1853 to
Ibadan. Before 1850, the Baptists were also active in Yorubaland. In the delta area the first missionaries were from the
Church of Scotland and they established themselves at Calabar
in 1846. Their success there can be measured by the abolition
of human sacrifice by the Egbo Society only four years after
the opening of the mission. In 1858 at the death of the King
of Creek Town, not one slave was sacrificed. Despite this local
achievement, missionaries were not welcomed in the other major
coastal towns. However, some stations were established on the
Cross River. The third major arena for missionary activity was
in the lands bordering the Niger River. The links between commercial activity and missionaries were more obvious there than
elsewhere in Nigeria. The Reverend Samuel Crowther, who had
been on the ill-fated 1841 expedition, was placed in charge of
the Niger mission. Crowther and the Reverend J. C. Taylor,
also an African, accompanied Dr. Baikie on the *Dayspring* in
1857 to select suitable mission sites. Three stations were estab-

lished, one at Onitsha, one at Gbebe, and one at Lokoja. Of these only the Onitsha Mission proved successful.

Despite the hostility of many African rulers and traders, the missionaries of all denominations slowly advanced their cause. A number of nonreligious factors aided them. Perhaps the most important in the period after 1860 was the increased activity by the British Government in areas that previously had been relatively untouched by British influence. The missionaries also brought education and many Africans saw in this a way to advance their children's future in a rapidly changing world. Much of the early missionary activity had been carried on by Africans, typically freed slaves who had been educated in Sierra Leone. Samuel Crowther, who became the Bishop of "Western Equatorial Africa beyond the Queen's Dominions" in 1864, is the best example of the influence of Christian Africans upon Nigeria. The high proportion of African missionaries obviously helped convince non-Christian Africans of the efficacy of the new faith and that they too could learn the white man's ways.

It should be noted that despite the success of European merchants and missionaries in their interior ventures, there had been little real penetration of the Eastern hinterland. Mission and trading stations were concentrated along the coast or adjacent to the Niger River. In the 1870's, further attempts by merchants to dispense with African middlemen led to a series of conflicts in the coast towns as the rulers attempted to maintain their favored position and deny further interior access to the Europeans. Perhaps the most serious development in this period was the rise of King Jaja's power at Opobo and the subsequent negation of Bonny as the dominant delta town. After 1865, Bonny was divided into two factions, one supporting Oko-Jumbo, a former slave and now chief adviser to the new king, while the other backed Jaja, also a former slave. Civil war broke out in 1869 and Jaja, realizing his weaknesses, led his followers into Andoni country and established the town of Opobo. From there he could cut Bonny's supply of oil products. By the end of 1870, fourteen of the eighteen houses of Bonny had declared allegiance to the new state and Bonny's real power was at an end.[16] Henceforth Jaja dominated delta politics.

Further to the west in Warri, the British, after 1851, had sought to keep the Benin River open for trade by making agreements with the Itsekiri rulers. The rulers agreed to choose from their numbers one man who would act as governor of the river. However, there were factionalism and genuine fears of the growing British interests on the river. One governor, Chanomi, was removed by the British in 1879 for blocking trade, and in 1884, Governor Nana placed a part of his territory under British protection. European rivalries and Nana's fears of losing everything made the Benin River, after Opobo, one of the main areas of native resistance to British encroachments in the 1890's.[17] Another important coast trading town disturbed by European activities of the 1880's was Brass. It, too, felt its importance waning and wished to stop the British advance.[18]

As previously indicated, British Government policy after 1850 was ambivalent. The official position which would remain in effect through the mid-1880's was to avoid territorial expansion which would imply an organized government structure and needless expense to the British taxpayer. Perhaps the best statement of this policy was the Report of the Select Committee of 1865.[19] On the other hand, the antislavery movement, missionary activity, and growing economic commitment meant that Government could not maintain a completely hands-off attitude. In 1849 there was only one consul for all the coastal areas of Nigeria. In 1851 a vice-consul was appointed for Lagos, becoming a full consul two years later. In 1861, Lagos was annexed and the British representative was designated a lieutenant governor. In the next few years vice-consuls would be appointed to some of the more important trading states. These men were more than representatives of the British Government. They actively intervened in the internal affairs of the African states and called for assistance from the Navy when needed. By the late 1870's, stated policy notwithstanding, the British had a *de facto* protectorate over the most important coastal areas. Britain's contradictory attitude could be maintained because British interests in Nigeria had been relatively unchallenged by any other European power.

Beginning in the late 1870's French merchants backed by

expansionist-minded goverments became extremely active in West Africa. The threat to British interests increased when the Germans entered the race in the early 1880's. Thus Britain's trade hegemony was threatened. In all probability, given the nonexpansionist attitude of the British Government, much of Nigeria would have been lost had it not been for the activities of George Goldie Taubman (later Sir George Taubman Goldie).[20]

Arriving in Nigeria in 1877 to settle family business interests, Goldie found the Niger trade fragmented among a number of small competitive firms. By 1879 he had convinced the directors of competitive companies that by joining him in the newly formed United Africa Company they could secure greater profits and also be better protected against French competition. Goldie's aim was a monopoly of the Niger trade. However, two French companies, the *Compagnie Française de l'Afrique Équatoriale* and the *Compagnie du Sénégal et de la Côte Occidental d'Afrique,* together had assets almost equal to Goldie's company. In 1882, faced with evidence of increased French interest in West Africa, Goldie began to press the British Government to grant his newly re-formed company, the National African Company, a royal charter. In this way Britain could secure an effective protectorate over the Niger territories without incurring the expense normally associated with a protectorate. The Government refused Goldie's requests but did grant him the right to make treaties with native rulers.

The National African Company launched a trade war against its French rivals and drove them out of business by 1884. Goldie by that time had made thirty-seven treaties with local rulers and these became, at the Congress of Berlin, major factors in excluding France and Germany from the Niger. The company also maintained a fleet of gunboats to assure its dominance on the river. A charter was granted to the National African Company in 1886, giving it political authority in those areas where the company had treaties with native rulers. In 1887, these company territories came under British protection and the name of the company was changed to the Royal Niger Company.[21] The company agents, however, were supposed to interfere as little as possible in native affairs except to further trade and complete the abolition of slavery. The company was further enjoined to allow freedom of trade to all its competitors.

Meanwhile in 1885, in response to the German takeover in the Cameroon, Britain had proclaimed the Oil River Protectorate over the territory from Lagos east to the Cameroon.[22] On paper the Foreign Office, through its Consul for the Bight of Benin, controlled a protectorate extending into the interior as far as the Benue River. Actually any effective British authority over the hinterland came not from the inadequate power of its consuls, but from the Royal Niger Company. Britain did not establish the machinery for effective government of the protectorate until 1891. Despite the weakness of their positions in the interior, Consul Hewitt and his successor, H. H. Johnston, in conjunction with the merchants, brought the coastal towns more firmly under British authority.

The most dramatic victory of the British along the coast in this period was over King Jaja of Opobo. Pressed by the company's agents and European merchants based on the coast, Jaja attempted to prevent their direct contacts with the sources of his trading monopoly. How far he would go to defend himself is seen in his punitive expedition against the Kwa Ibo in 1881. The Kwa Ibo had been foolish enough to allow Europeans to build factories in their towns and to trade directly with them. Jaja sent fifty war canoes against the Kwa Ibo, destroyed the factories, and slaughtered many prisoners. The Berlin Conference had assigned Jaja's territories to Britain whose government ostensibly believed in free trade. A clash between free trade and Jaja's protectionist activities became inevitable. In 1887, Consul Johnston, backed by gunboats, decided to end Jaja's obstruction. Tricking the King into a conference, Johnston seized him and shipped him to Accra for trial. Jaja was subsequently exiled, on pension, to the West Indies.[23]

This action against Jaja was unusual for the consuls of the Oil Rivers did not have the funds or military forces to pursue such an activist policy against all hostile rulers ostensibly under their control. Those rulers were rendered relatively impotent, however, by the actions of the Royal Niger Company.

From its headquarters at Asaba on the Niger, the company attempted to establish, despite the provisions of its charter, an effective monopoly. The company had formed a large administrative body to run the territories under its control. To make this effective there was a constabulary and a fleet of gunboats. The northern limits of the company's holdings were undefined. Goldie was afraid of a French takeover of the middle Niger. These two facts, combined with the desire for profits, dictated a forward policy of forcing native rulers to accept economic and political decisions made by the company.

The company's policy was slowly strangling the once important coastal towns and creating problems which in the 1890's would have to be solved by the consuls. For the British government, however, the most important sphere of activity of the company was its political takeover in west-central Nigeria in order to thwart French designs on Borgu. This culminated in the so-called race to Nikki in 1894 which nearly became an international incident. Later the company conquered Nupe and Ilorin. After 1896, a more imperialistic British Government discovered that, whatever services the company had performed in the past, it was at a disadvantage when in competition with the French Government. Thus in 1898, Britain authorized the creation of an imperial military force to hold the territory gained by the company. The need to restrict French encroachments on the Niger, combined with a growing chorus of complaints by merchants of the monopolistic practices of the company, impelled the Government to take over the company. After long negotiations this was finally accomplished when all the company's territories were transferred to the Crown in January 1900.[24]

It is important to note that the main thrust of company activity had been along the Niger River and north and west from Lokoja. Obviously its economic policies affected not only the delta and coast people, but also those of the immediate hinterland. However, except on the fringes, company agents had not even penetrated the Ibo lands. The same ignorance of the Ibo hinterland prevailed among the officials of the Oil

Rivers Protectorate, for their main interest in the 1891–1896 period was in establishing British control along the coast.

In 1891, Major Claude MacDonald was appointed Consul General of the reorganized Oil Rivers Protectorate with a small staff of vice-consuls, an embryo civil service, and an armed force of less than two hundred men. The Oil Rivers Protectorate was renamed the Niger Coast Protectorate in 1893, and MacDonald was designated High Commissioner. One of Mac-Donald's main tasks was to fight the amalgamation of Protectorate territories with those of the company. His belief in free trade made him an opponent of the restrictive practices not only of the coastal rulers but also of the company. MacDonald also disagreed with the use of military force to crush native opposition.[25] In this he was out of step with his time because it was too late to repair the damage done to good relations between Europeans and natives. Even had there been no compelling economic and political reasons for crushing native opposition, humanitarian pressures in Britain would have forced him to take definite action against human sacrifice, slavery, and the slave trade.

Three major crises faced MacDonald and his chief lieutenant, Ralph Moor, in their attempts to extend peacefully the actual scope of Protectorate rule. The first occurred in 1893 when an Akuna chief brought trade to a standstill on the Cross River. The newly formed constabulary ended the threat and the chief was tried for murder and hanged.[26] More important was the reaction in 1894 of Nana, leader of the Itsekiri, to the Commissioner's attempts to open his hinterland for free trade. Nana had created a monopoly of the trade on the Benin River and was also dealing in slaves. The acting vice-consul, Ralph Moor, who was much more of an activist than Mac-Donald, precipitated a conflict with Nana by summoning him to answer various charges. Nana refused and also ignored a further order forbidding his men to trade on the Benin River. In September 1894, Moor, using four gunboats, the constabulary, and men of the regular Navy, stormed Nana's strong point of Brohemie and captured large amounts of trade goods as well as many guns. Nana later gave himself up; he was tried and deported to the Gold Coast.[27]

The third conflict during MacDonald's period did not at first concern actions by the Protectorate Government but was caused by the monopolistic practices of the company. The traders of Brass were outside the company's jurisdiction and were therefore treated as foreigners, each being required to pay heavy fees for the privilege of trading in company territory. The Brassmen tried every means short of war to modify these restrictions, which would inevitably strangle their state. In January 1895, their desperation was so great that they took the company port of Akassa and destroyed the trade goods there. From the European viewpoint the crime was compounded by the capture of sixty Africans, a number of whom were eaten later by the Brassmen. Although MacDonald was sympathetic to the economic plight of Brass, he could not ignore this attack against the company made by natives under his jurisdiction. A punitive force was dispatched to Nembe, the major town of the Brassmen and against fierce resistance the town was eventually taken and burned.[28]

All of the traditional centers of trade along the coast had submitted to British authority by the time Moor succeeded MacDonald as Consul General in 1896. The only great kingdom of southern Nigeria which lay outside effective British control was that of once-mighty Benin. Benin had retreated into self-imposed isolation, giving way to orgies of human sacrifice to propitiate the gods. In 1892, the king (*Oba*) had agreed to place Benin under British protection and to abolish slavery and human sacrifice. However, when Vice-Consul J. B. Phillips left for Benin in 1897, presumably to overawe the Binis into complying with the treaty, he and the major portion of his native escort were killed. In less than six weeks a punitive expedition took Benin, burned the town, and carried away as spoils thousands of the best examples of Benin sculpture. The Oba was later captured and exiled to Calabar.[29] With the destruction of Benin, the Protectorate Government could turn its energies toward establishing effective machinery for governing the territory. Further, it could give serious consideration to bringing the

Ibo and Ibibio people of the interior under actual rather than theoretical control.

Sir Claude MacDonald,[30] after his difficulties with Nana, had planned to concentrate in 1895 on the peaceful penetration of Iboland. Despite inadequate information concerning the Ibo, MacDonald did not make the mistake of believing that he would be dealing with a single, comprehensive state. He requested the Foreign Office to send him five hundred treaty forms. The African Department could not understand why so many were needed and the Consul had to explain that the Ibo did not recognize paramount chiefs and that unless the Foreign Office would be satisfied with a mere declaration of a protectorate over the area, he would need all the forms.[31] MacDonald's understanding that Iboland was not chaotic, despite the lack of paramount chiefs, and his desire for peaceful penetration of the interior went for nothing. The attack by the Brassmen against Akassa diverted his attention in 1895, and in the following year he was succeeded as Consul General by his more aggressive deputy, Ralph Moor.

Moor, who deserves to be numbered among the foremost architects of the British Empire in Africa, has been overshadowed by his two contemporaries, Sir George Goldie and Frederick Lugard. In the formative period of British administration in Nigeria, however, Moor was perhaps more important than either of them. Goldie's star was waning along with the fortunes of the Royal Niger Company, and Lugard's major contributions were yet to come. Moor, a very complex man, directed the final conquest of southern Nigeria and the creation of a viable administration on the basis of certain assumptions. He was opposed to the company because of its restrictive trade practices and fought its very real or imagined attempt to take over Protectorate territory. Moor believed in the "dual mandate" long before it was given literary form by Lugard. He was disgusted by such native practices as human sacrifice, cannibalism, and twin killing, and he wished to make effective the ban on slavery and slave trading. All this he believed could be accomplished under a firm and fair British administration. Trade must come first and then all the other advantages of the Pax

Britannica would follow. Moor welcomed peaceful integration, but all of his dealings with Africans were based on the assumption that only he was right. If Africans accepted his conclusions all would be well, if not he would use force to crush any opposition. By 1898, Moor had the power to begin the conquest of the interior and he had learned much from the punitive expeditions of the Royal Niger Company.[32]

Moor's administrative and judicial reforms will be detailed later; it is sufficient to state here that these occupied much of the time of the Consul and his small staff. This was particularly true after June 1899, when the southern portion of the territories of the company passed to the Crown. This much larger area was renamed the Protectorate of Southern Nigeria and Moor was appointed High Commissioner.[33] Moor's preoccupation with administrative details caused his early-stated goal of pacifying the interior to be postponed. There were also other factors. Ignorance about the interior peoples was one. For example, the first European to visit Bende in Aro country was Vice-Consul Leonard in 1896. It would have been precipitous for Moor to act before obtaining some intelligence of the land and people. Even when Moor did act definitely, his major weakness was the basing of erroneous assumptions upon inadequate information. Another factor that deterred Moor from moving rapidly into Iboland was the lack of sufficient troops.

Despite the small size of the constabulary available, Moor sanctioned a number of punitive expeditions against natives on the periphery of territory actually controlled by the administration. The first of these after the Benin expedition was directed in early 1898 against the peoples of the upper reaches of the Cross River where a small force met fierce resistance from Ekuri, Asiga, and Ibo, and accomplished very little. Another expedition in April and May 1898, in the central division, achieved considerable success on the fringes of Ibo country. Chiefs in the Benin area continued to be troublesome and a number of expeditions were required before the rebellious chiefs were disposed of in mid-1899. In February 1899, a major thrust into Kwa Ibo country north of Opobo resulted in the destruction of nine villages and the submission of 175 others.[34]

Despite such activity, Moor had not suceeded by 1900 in making much impact on the hinterland of Opobo, Bonny, or Degema, had no foothold at all in the area of the upper Cross River, and still had the wide territory of Iboland to deal with. Moor, however, believed in the efficacy of military expeditions, and as he considered the problem of bringing Iboland under control, the pieces of the complex puzzle fell into place. A major military force aimed at the destruction of Aro power would eliminate what he considered the major political obstacle to British advance in Iboland. If successful, this thrust would outflank the still recalcitrant chiefs further to the south. The Colonial Office, dominated by the expansionist policies of Chamberlain, agreed.

Moor and his staff also knew very little of the Aro and their peculiar position among the Ibo. They considered the Aro as a militaristic people who held the Ibo in subjection in much the same fashion as the Ashanti of the Gold Coast controlled less powerful native tribes. This erroneous assumption ascribed to the Aro a power that they never possessed. More important, it meant that all of Moor's plans for British hegemony over Iboland were predicted on the necessity of crushing Aro military power. The Aro did have a peculiar position among the Ibo, but they did not retain this because of military prowess or an effective centralized government. They were great traders and had their agents throughout Iboland. They held a virtual monopoly as middlemen between the up-country natives and the coast and also had effective military alliances with people such as the Ada and Abam who were used to punish villages that refused tribute or otherwise were dangers to the confederation. The Aro did not devise any political structure for Iboland. They did not attempt to establish Aro rulers in the Ibo towns nor did they try to consolidate the scattered villages into larger kingdoms. The greatest hold which the Aro had over the Ibo was the control of "Chukwu" or the Long Juju, the most famous shrine in all Nigeria. Although the Aro were an important factor in Iboland, they never had the kind of influence attributed to them by the British.[35]

Moor and his associates had decided that the Aro were

the main threat to British occupation of the interior. This perhaps explains why no treaties with any major Ibo group had been concluded before the Aro Expedition. In 1900, Moor began the military build-up for the overthrow of the Aro. The Ashanti War siphoned off a large number of men scheduled for the expedition, and it was not until the following year that the expedition could get under way. Troops were sent from Lagos and from Lugard's command in the north. By the time Lieutenant Colonel Montanaro was ready to move against the Aro, his command was composed of 87 officers, 1,550 soldiers, and 2,100 carriers. In November 1901, Moor explained to Chamberlain, the Colonial Secretary, what he hoped to achieve by the expedition. His aims were to halt the slave trade and domestic slavery, establish a labor market in place of slavery, abolish the Juju hierarchy of the Aro, and open the hinterland for legitimate trade and civilization. The Colonial Office had previously given its blessing to the undertaking and operations were begun in December.[36]

Montanaro had grouped his forces at four stations as the basis of a four-pronged thrust into Aro territory. These were at Unwana and Itu on the Cross River, Akwette, and Oguta. The Oguta and Akwette columns joined at Owerri and then marched on Bende which was reached on December 16. The Itu and Unwana columns arrived at Aro-Chuku on the 24th and entered the town without opposition. Four days later the columns from Bende joined them. There was little opposition from the supposedly savage Aro, partly because the Aro, despite the evidence of British preparation in 1901, seemed unaware that they were to be attacked. Montanaro, not to be outdone by his colleagues in the recent Ashanti War, issued bulletins for the benefit of the High Commissioner in which he exaggerated the opposition.[37] For all the British fears and their cautious military preparation, the campaign was a tame affair. Most of the serious clashes came when the people in the occupied towns refused to surrender their guns as demanded.

The Aro Expedition, although falling short of the expectations of the military, did succeed in establishing British authority throughout much of the interior. In all the Ibo towns through which the columns passed, the people could see British power—many for the first time. This was particularly true in such places as Oguta, Owerri, and Bende where Montanaro placed large numbers of troops. The Aro confederation was broken and the Long Juju destroyed. Obviously this had a positive psychological effect upon the Ibo and their potential resistance to the British. In March 1902, Moor visited the interior and Aro. One company of the Southern Nigerian Regiment was established at Aba and one at Owerri, preparatory to making these places district headquarters. At Bende, Moor gave instructions to the political officers to establish Native Courts. Military detachments were later posted at Asaba, Oguta, Sabagreira, and Ido. Advised by political officers, they were to be used against recalcitrant towns and as the major means for "peaceful penetration." [38]

The degree to which military force was later utilized depended upon the condition of a specific area and the personal whim of the political officer. Some, such as W. Fosbery, disdained the use of force, preferring rather to work at mollifying the distrust of the people. Others used force continually to assure obedience to their orders. No large-scale military expeditions were used after the Aro venture. Rather, small patrols from the military stations fanned out into districts not yet controlled or where there seemed to be hostility. Some of the most important of these operations were against the Ngor area north of Owerri and the Asaba hinterland in 1902,[39] into Afikpo country in 1903,[40] the Onitsha hinterland in 1904,[41] and the Noria-Ovoro patrol and operations in the Cross River in 1905.[42] As Moor and his successor, Sir Walter Egerton, viewed them, the patrols were quasi-political and their major function was to overawe the populace so that they would accept the new political system. These patrols continued even after 1906 when Southern Nigeria was joined to the Colony and Protectorate of Lagos.

By the close of Moor's tenure as High Commissioner, Britain's control of the hinterland, although not completed, was assured. One long-held opinion, that the occupation of southern Nigeria was reluctant and hesitant, is false. Once the British Government had reversed its stand on expansion and had assumed sovereignty from the Royal Niger Company, the conquest of the eastern section was militarily as swift and sure as Lugard's more highly publicized northern venture.

CHAPTER III

The Establishment of British Control

Attempting to resolve the question of the best and cheapest method of consolidating British rule in the Oil Rivers, the Foreign Office in early 1889 sent Major Claude MacDonald to investigate and report on conditions there. More specifically, MacDonald was to consider the possibility of allowing the Royal Niger Company to assume responsibility for the coastal areas. If MacDonald reported against such a proposition, he was to inform the Foreign Secretary what he considered the best alternatives. Should the Oil Rivers be annexed to the Colony of Lagos, should the region have a separate colonial administration, or should the existing consular type of government be continued?[1] MacDonald arrived in the Oil Rivers in March and for the next two months traveled to all the major coastal towns. He talked with chiefs, British officials, and merchants, and in June 1889 made his report to the Foreign Office.[2]

In this comprehensive account, MacDonald noted the hostility of all the most important native rulers toward the Royal Niger Company and confirmed the opposition of the Liverpool traders to such a move. He believed that the Oil Rivers was

E

rich enough to support crown-colony government, but in his opinion it would be premature to attempt its establishment immediately. Accordingly MacDonald strongly recommended the continuance of the consular form, strengthened, however, to provide the first step in establishing direct British control over the protected states. Salisbury, over the objections of some of his advisers, approved MacDonald's report and commissioned him, prior to his appointment as Consul General, to draft the design for the stronger consular establishment. After almost a year of discussions with the Treasury, MacDonald's amended plan was approved. This called for a Consul General and Commissioner, six vice-consuls, and a small executive establishment. In July 1891, MacDonald and his vice-consuls arrived at Bonny empowered by an Order in Council of 1889 to legislate by means of proclamations for the renamed Niger Coast Protectorate.[3]

However minuscule this establishment was, it represented a radical change in the attitude of the Foreign Office toward the territory. Under the pressure of events described in Chapter II, the size of the civil and military establishment quickly grew and the area of British jurisdiction within a decade included most of the hinterland. MacDonald did away with the "comey" system of payments which chiefs used to gain revenue, and established a regular scale of import and export duties. These tariffs provided the means of financing the administration and also enabled the British to convert the chiefs into agents of the administration by means of money payments. In 1895, the Protectorate was reorganized administratively in order to secure more readily the pacification of the hinterland. This regrouping established three districts—eastern, central, and western. Calabar, the headquarters of the eastern section, was to be concerned with the incorporation of the upper Cross River areas; Okikra and Opobo were to be the springboards for advances into Ibo territory; and officials at Warri were to be concerned with the kingdom of Benin.

MacDonald resurrected an earlier plan of H. H. Johnston which established Native Councils. This was an attempt to utilize formally the services of chiefs who had influence in the coast cities. By mid-1892, Native Councils were functioning at Bonny, Buguma, and Degema.[4] These councils had limited legislative and judicial powers in the towns. In the outlying districts, MacDonald created minor courts staffed by natives and ostensibly devoted to administering traditional law. In 1892, the High Court of the Native Council of Old Calabar was created, which acted as an appeal court from the Native Councils. In addition there were the Consular Courts which in many cases acted as first courts of appeal. For the first few years of the operation of the Protectorate courts, there was not a clear separation between the Native Courts and the British court system. This would not be brought about until 1899.

Nevertheless, the seeds of later difficulties were present in these establishments, which were created by the British to advance their control of the country. The Native Councils and minor courts carried out the vice-consul's instructions while the High Court at Old Calabar was manipulated by the Commissioner, particularly by Ralph Moor, MacDonald's successor. Chiefs or even kings were removed from the councils when they opposed British policy too openly. A particularly flagrant example of this was the removal of King Amachree of New Calabar from that council in 1897.[5] Here indeed was an anomaly—a council supposedly mirroring in some part the traditional system, functioning without its King. In the previous year the formation of the Native Council at Okikra followed the deportation of King Koko of Nembe-Brass. The major reason for the creation of the council was to eliminate the influence of the King, who had been hostile to Europeans. A more telling case for the nonnative origins of the councils concerned Benin. Even before the capture of the Oba, the British representative formed a Native Council of chiefs who had early submitted to British authority. In June 1899, the Oba was captured and brought before this new council which had already made significant changes in "native" law to suit the High Commissioner. Not surprisingly, the King was found to have violated "native" law and custom.[6] Thus even in territories where presumably the authorities knew something of traditional social and political forms, the pressure of conquest allowed them to establish councils that were nothing but creatures of British administration.

In 1899, H. L. Galway proposed to the High Commissioner a series of proclamations intended to clarify the distinctions among the various courts.[7] However, nothing was done at this time, partly because of the necessity of establishing more Native Councils, but particularly because of the crisis in the house system. British interference with trade and politics had loosened the ties that bound the "boys" to the heads of "houses." Thus it appeared to Moor that one of the most stabilizing influences along the coast was falling apart. In response to this threat, Moor issued a proclamation in 1899 which he hoped would help maintain the position of the heads of houses.[8] Two years later a more encompassing House Rule Proclamation was issued which made it an offense with severe penalties for a member of a house to challenge the authority of the head.[9] These enactments can be considered as pragmatic solutions for real problems. However, they betray the authorities' substantial lack of knowledge of the native peoples. The second House Rule Proclamation was to apply to the whole of the Protectorate since it was presumed that this institution was characteristic of all peoples including the Ibibio and Ibo. The fact that no serious attempt was made to make the proclamation work in the hinterland does not negate the original presumption that it was an effective proclamation.

In June 1899 the southern territories controlled by the Royal Niger Company passed to the Crown, tremendously increasing—at least in theory—the area under the jurisdiction of Sir Ralph Moor.[10] This addition made imperative the rationalization of the mechanisms of British rule in the enlarged Protectorate. Despite the objections of the commercial community, the royal instructions to Moor in January 1900 on governing the renamed Protectorate of Southern Nigeria made no provision for an executive or legislative council.[11] All powers acquired by the Crown were vested in the High Commissioner. Ultimate responsibility for administering the area passed from the Foreign Office to the Colonial Office. Although his European staff was far from adequate for the tasks involved, Moor believed that British rule should be absolute and be distinct from that of traditional rulers. In minor administrative work the native system could be utilized, subject always to revision and control. Thus from the beginning Moor's assumptions regarding sovereignty were at variance with what later was supposed to be the basis of British rule—the use of traditional institutions to govern subject peoples. Moor would utilize native authorities as he understood them, but only in subordinate capacities and always subject to management and veto by British administrators.[12]

The earlier political division of the Protectorate was maintained but with the addition of a fourth division—that of the Cross River. Later, in December 1902, Old Calabar was made a fifth division to function directly under the chief secretary.[13] Each of these divisions was then subdivided into districts and subdistricts under the jurisdiction of district commissioners or assistant district commissioners. The area of most of these districts extended approximately two days' march (about thirty miles) from the district station, and each district commissioner had control over 1,500–2,000 square miles.[14] These early districts bore little relation to the unity of the people within them. They were established quite arbitrarily with the main purpose of creating a manageable block of territory that the district commissioner could control. Even later, after the growth of the civil staff, district boundaries were laid out with little reference to the people. The boundaries of the districts and, more importantly, native-court areas would include groups with different political and social practices and traditions. Backing up the civil administration at this time was the Third Niger Battalion under the command of Colonel Montanaro and the civil police. This latter group comprised the court messengers and forty men who previously had served the Royal Niger Company. A regular police force was created in 1902 to assume responsibility previously exercised by the military.[15]

Moor had no intention of recognizing existing political forms or creating new ones that could challenge or modify the political supremacy of British officials. Nevertheless, it was necessary with such a small staff to have some agency in the occupied area that could maintain law and order and dispense justice on a continuing basis. The High Commissioner found the solution to this set of problems by utilizing the rather new Native Courts. By issuing warrants to certain presumed traditional leaders to sit on these courts the British were able to create a legal structure which also had administrative ramifications. For these "warrant chiefs" became the medium through which orders from the British were passed on to the people. However suspect such an arrangement was when it was first instituted among people who were governed by chiefs, it became really destructive of traditional values and leadership when applied to people who were not governed by chiefs. Moor and later Egerton and their advisers were not overly troubled by this potential of their proclamations. At first Moor presumed that the native political structures observable along the coast were· also present in the interior. Later when it became obvious that the Ibo's political system was village oriented without chiefs, the Ibo were dismissed as backward and their territories considered to be always in a state of anarchy.[16] Thus the British could congratulate themselves that their Native Courts Proclamations made provisions for the establishment of order and stability. By providing these all but leaderless people with ready-made chiefs, the British believed they were bringing them up to the standards of more advanced African people.

The Protectorate Government reorganized the courts so that they could act in the interior as the major means to control the population. A proclamation in 1900 established a two-tiered system of Native Courts.[17] At the lowest level were minor courts, which were directed by a "native authority" which was in every case a chief. Superior to these were the Native Councils which were all located at district headquarters and were presided over by British political officers. In both types of courts the personnel of the court were chosen by the High Commissioner or his representative and warrants of appointment were issued. These court members could be removed only by the British. Usually the district commissioner chose as members of the courts natives whom he believed represented traditional authority or in many cases men who would not oppose the wishes of the district commissioner.

The minor courts consisting of a president, vice-president, and four members had jurisdiction in civil matters involving up to £25 in cases of debt or £50 for inheritance. Native Council cases were limited to those not exceeding £200. The Native Councils had the power as well as theoretically the duty of supervising the minor courts. Although native law was supposed to guide the actions of both courts, the district commissioner had the real power. He could intervene at any stage of proceedings to transfer a case to a higher level, to annul the decision, or to order a new trial. The High Commissioner retained the ultimate power of withdrawing the right of any Native Court to function or to remove any member from the court.

Each Native Court had a clerk whose functions were to prepare the list of cases, call members for court sittings, issue summonses, keep records of the sitting, make sure the judgment book was signed, and keep a record of intake and disbursement of all moneys by the court. The clerk's duties were specialized and tedious but they demanded that he be able to read and write some English at a time when writing carried overtones of magic for most natives. Many of the illiterate warrant chiefs were overawed by the clerk's functions and abilities. Because of their skills in English, the clerks very early were transformed from mere servants of the court to the *de facto* masters.

The Proclamation of 1900 had been issued in a great hurry because of the addition of the southern portion of the Royal Niger territories to the Protectorate. It was almost immediately amended by another Native Courts Proclamation designed to make the system more functional.[18] There was no major alteration in the provisions of the previous act although some of the minor changes were to have important consequences for the system. The proclamation allowed the district commissioner to appoint a warrant chief to deputize for him as president of a Native Council. Although this provision was designed to relieve pressures on the overworked district commissioners, it gave lazy ones the opportunity to neglect their duty of supervising the courts. The proclamation also brought the Native Courts to a limited extent under the jurisdiction of the Supreme Court. In cases where the punishment was over £5 or imprisonment for over three months, appeal was authorized to the Supreme Court. Clerks of the court were required to send in monthly returns to the Judicial Department through the district commissioner's office where more detailed explanatory comments on each case were to be added.

A most important section of the Proclamation of 1901 made it illegal for any agency other than a Native Authority to exercise jurisdiction in any place where there was a functioning Native Court. Thus even before the occupation of the interior, Moor had established a rule which undermined the authority of the traditional hinterland rulers. From the first application of the proclamation dates the ambivalent pattern of the native-authority system. The warrant chiefs of a Native Court chosen by the British were vested with legal authority while the actual traditional rulers, however depleted their powers, were looked to by the people for continuing leadership.

In both Native Courts Proclamations, provision was made for court messengers. These functionaries were to serve process papers or to carry executive messages for the district commissioner and the court. In 1902 their duties were better defined in the hope of minimizing physical conflict upon the presentation of a summons. They were to report directly to the warrant chiefs for instructions before attempting to serve a summons.[19] Strict penalties were imposed upon persons interfering with or ignoring a court messenger. With the passage of time the official of the court who controlled the court messenger was not the warrant chief but the clerk of the court and this further increased the latter's assumed power.

In 1900, the apex of all court systems was the Supreme Court which consisted of a Chief Justice and one Pusine Judge. In the same year a Legal Department was created by the appointment of an attorney general. Another innovation introduced to the courts system in 1900 was Special Commissioner's Courts operating in troubled areas which would have concurrent jurisdiction with the Supreme Court.[20] In the following year a "traveling supervisor" was appointed to examine and report on the accounts and records of the Native Courts.[21] The traveling supervisor was attached to the Judicial Department until 1905. Moor considered this office most important in making certain the Native Courts, the bulwark of his administration, functioned properly.

Despite the difficulties and the small European staff available, there were seventy-two courts operating by 1903, and they had heard 2,986 criminal and 17,000 civil cases.[22] Such statistics do not mean what observers may read into them—that because large numbers of cases were handled, the system was therefore functioning well. What it does indicate is the speed of Moor's lieutenants in establishing a court system which in many ways was a negation of previous native law and procedure. One obvious reason for the initial success lay in the use of force or the threat of force implied in the conquest of the interior.

In August 1902, Justice M. Menendez was instructed by Moor to visit, inspect, and reorganize, if necessary the Native Courts of the central, eastern and western divisions.[23] Although Menendez, after visiting forty-one courts, was critical of some portions of the system, his report was generally laudatory. His conclusion that the system was "excellent" and without parallel in West Africa" convinced Moor that his policies were correct. Further, any modification of the system until Lugard became Governor-General was in general agreement with Menendez's and Moor's evaluations.

The most important factors in the decision to extend the native courts system into the hinterland were the speed of conquest of Iboland and the type of political officers then serving the government. Despite the fact that many military expeditions were later directed against the Ibo, the year 1903 marked the effective takeover of most of the interior. After the Aro Expedition, military and political officers found little organized Ibo resistance. This meant that some type of government had to be established immediately among these strange, almost stateless people. Although the theory was to maintain traditional forms so far as possible, the Government was already predisposed to believe that there were chiefs or even kings among the Ibo.

There was little time even had the Government been more concerned, to learn the complex social and political arrangements of the Ibo. Thus Moor sanctioned the imposition upon the Ibo of the native courts system, as defined by the Proclamation of 1901.

Political officers who served in the Protectorate were most unusual men. They were called upon to face the unhealthy climate, loneliness, and physical dangers in many forms. They needed health, stamina, coolness in the face of danger, and a sense of supreme confidence in themselves. However laudable were these qualities, many officers were new to West Africa and were certainly unfamiliar with the peoples of the hinterland. Most could not speak even the languages of the coast and could converse with the Ibo only through interpreters who more often than not told them what they believed the white man wanted to hear. They had never been trained in anything as esoteric as the newly emergent discipline of anthropology. Although not despising the native, they were convinced of his inferiority. Much of their self-confidence came from an almost single-minded belief that British virtues were the best and that their major purpose was to share, if only in small degree, these blessings with the poor African. British administrators in the early twentieth century were rulers, not men prepared to search out patiently the mainsprings of a society as complex as the Ibo.

In 1904, Sir Walter Egerton became High Commissioner of the Protectorate of Southern Nigeria. He also acted after September of that year as the administrator of Lagos Colony and continued Moor's forward policy of military pacification. Between October 1904 and June 1905, there were eight separate field operations. After the conclusion of these campaigns, Egerton established seven new Government stations, each with a resident political officer.[24] Aside from this pacification, Egerton's most important contribution was in arranging the amalgamation of the Niger Coast Protectorate with the Colony of Lagos.[25] Fiscal union and a subsequent saving of money was the primary objective of the Colonial Office in urging this merger. The new Protectorate of Southern Nigeria of necessity had a larger and

more sophisticated administrative structure and Lagos became
the administrative center of the Protectorate. The title of High
Commissioner was dropped and that of Governor was substituted. The Governor was to be assisted by a lieutenant governor
who also functioned as the chief secretary. The Protectorate
was divided into three provinces—the Western, Central and
Eastern—each under a "provincial commissioner." Each provincial commissioner was to be all but autonomous, largely
because of difficulties in communication. Only the most important matters had to be referred to Lagos for confirmation. Despite this, the amalgamation was tantamount to a down grading
of the eastern sections. Instead of a High Commissioner resident
at Calabar, henceforth there would be only a provincial commissioner. The Governor, far removed in Lagos, became more
concerned with the practical difficulties of the easier-to-reach
Yoruba West. This in itself contributed to the isolation and
future neglect of the interests of the Ibo and Ibibio peoples.

The creation of the larger Protectorate necessitated a new
statement of native policy. Egerton and his chief advisers were
obviously satisfied with the functioning of the previous system,
even among the "backward" Ibo. Therefore the Native Courts
Proclamation of 1906 did not alter the major provisions of the
previous proclamations.[26] It substituted the provincial commissioner for the High Commissioner, making him responsible for
all courts and officers in the area under his jurisdiction. The
provincial commissioner, district commissioners, and assistant
district commissioners were introduced more directly into the
functioning of the Native Courts. Whenever they presided over
a minor court it automatically became a Native Council. The
rights of review of and interference into court activities and
decisions by British officials remained, and every Native Court
became subject to the orders of the Supreme Court. Every
month court clerks had to provide the Supreme Court with a
full list of criminal cases where the decision had involved payment of over £20 fine or three months in prison. This list acted
as an automatic appeal and the Supreme Court or any of its
Judges could on review, without argument, amend or annul

the previous order. Native Courts thus became after 1906 not just customary courts but the lowest level of a British court system.

This provision caused great headaches for everyone concerned and was one of the major points attacked by Lugard when he became Governor-General. First it provided more work for the clerks while at the same time it made them more important than ever before. The records of decisions to be passed on to the Supreme Court were supposed to be full enough to allow the Justices to render such decisions. This was seldom achieved even after the district commissioners had made notations amplifying the cases. Unless the British official had been present, he had no real knowledge of a particular case and the records provided by the court clerks were not sufficient to enlighten anyone in the higher echelons. Further, for the principle of review to be fully effective, a much larger Supreme Court would have been necessary. The court, which in 1912 had grown to four members, could not, even if it had wanted to, keep abreast of all the cases referred to it.

The real weakness of the native-court system prior to 1912 was the presupposition that the system of chiefs was universally applicable to the Eastern Province. The fact that the bulk of the people were unfamiliar with such a system rendered completely absurd the British arguments that they were following native tradition. The charge has long been made against the British that in those African territories which were accustomed to chiefs, they picked "yes men" who had no claim to rule. The accusation that Britain was more concerned with gaining compliant subordinates than in seeking out legitimate leaders becomes more valid when applied to the hinterlands of the Eastern Province. The fact that there were no traditional chiefs in this area was merely a challenge to the British to create them.

British authorities operated under the illusion that they were continuing native practices by choosing men whom they had identified as traditional leaders to be chiefs, whatever the sanctions for their rule. Regardless of this faulty premise, how were the warrant chiefs actually selected? There are no good records on the method of selection of the early warrant chiefs. We know, however, that after 1919, the methods used were quite arbitrary, with each political officer establishing his own criteria. Not until 1923 was there an order from higher echelons asking district commissioners to inquire into the traditional status of warrant chiefs and to report on the method of their selection. It is reasonable to believe that the early political officers were at least as arbitrary in their methods as were later officials.

What were the major difficulties in choosing warrant chiefs who had at least some sanction to rule? In the earliest days following conquest or occupation of an area, elders and headmen were afraid to expose themselves for fear of the new, powerful white men. In this period the native who could master his fear and become associated with or help the British could expect to be rewarded. Some of these men received warrants from their masters although they had no status in the village or town which they represented. Even after initial fears had passed there were still reasons why traditional rulers did not present themselves. There was a real concern that elders, if they accepted the role, would be forced to break taboos associated with their semisacred positions. In this connection not only the elders but the people sought to protect their leaders and their village from actions that might reflect upon their concept of the right society. The putting forward of men with little status was a matter of protection not only for the elders but also for all the people.[27]

When contact was first made with Europeans, many Ibo did not believe white men to be human because of their white skins, their boots, and their skill with guns. The military expeditions of the early years did nothing to ease the Ibo's fears. Such activities as burning of crops and villages and holding headmen hostages were all detrimental to feelings of trust. Villagers were not going to point out traditional leaders to the strange newcomers to have them suffer some unknown horrible fate. In some cases undesirables would be put forward to the British as leaders, believing that these men would either be killed or sold into slavery. Information on British activities passed quickly from village to village. Thus an action such as that of Galway's confiscation of a piece of very fertile land for district headquarters at Owerri was soon known throughout the territory. When elders from other villages heard how the traditional leaders at Owerri had been forced to surrender land, they were understandably reluctant to be placed in a similar position.[28]

Another important factor related to the selection of warrant chiefs was the difficulty of carrying out the duties. There were few courts, and the warrant chief, in order to earn his fee of five or even ten shillings per sitting, would have to travel many miles from his village. He might be called upon by the Commissioner to recruit laborers or carriers. In many cases this necessitated real physical exertion in chasing and catching those who didn't want to be recruited. Most of the traditional leaders were elders in a real and not just figurative sense and were not physically adequate for the position. Therefore, even when the actual headman was known to the British, they would often appoint a younger, stronger man to be "chief" in his place.[29]

From the beginning the only power and influence a warrant chief might have, even when called upon to exercise executive authority, rested on the fact that he possessed a "warrant" that made him a member of a Native Court. He depended upon the political officers and not native society for the retention of his position. As the Native Courts became more institutionalized, new symbols of the chief's authority began to appear. Reginald Hargrove, the district commissioner at Ikot-Ekpene, began the practice of giving fez-like caps and staffs surmounted by a crown to warrant chiefs and some headmen in his district. The practice soon spread throughout the Eastern Province and served to set the chief even further apart from his less fortunate townsmen.[30]

Warrant chiefs were given limited executive authority to see that orders from a political officer were carried out. All messages from higher authority were carried by court messengers to the court clerk. The clerk then either called in the warrant chief or sent a messenger to inform him of the order. Then the chief was supposed to carry out the order. In practice the chiefs divided their areas into wards over each of which they appointed a headman (*Ndumani*) who in fact carried out the orders of the political officer.[31] This innovation was not the result of Government decree but of practice and the political officers simply recognized it.

Apart from the problems already alluded to, the pre-1914 system of indirect rule had many other defects. One of the most serious was the method of judicial review established by the Proclamation of 1906. There were by 1912 forty-two Native Councils and forty-two minor courts in the Eastern Province.[32] It was physically impossible for four judges of the Supreme Court, in addition to their other duties, to review the pertinent cases from these courts. By 1912, there were 44,800 cases that needed to be reviewed.[33] The system, despite the stated opposition of the Government to Western trained lawyers' operating in the native courts, allowed such lawyers to represent clients appealing to the Supreme Court. This ran the litigant deeper into debt to the money lenders, many of whom were clerks of the Native Courts.

The provision in the Proclamation of 1901 that allowed European officers to appoint African deputies to act as presidents of the courts gave the district commissioners the excuse to absent themselves from meetings of the Native Councils. In Owerri, from June to September, 1914, there were eighty-nine sittings with the district commissioner present only twelve times. At Aba in the same period there were fifty-six sittings and the district commissioner was there only eight times.[34] This led even more to the domination of the court by the clerk. He understood more of the law than did the illiterate chiefs and in the continued absence of the European officers the chiefs came more and more under his direction. It also gave the clerks many more opportunities for overcharging on warrants and court fees and for collecting bribes. There were few ways to check upon income and disbursements of Native Courts since there was no standard method of keeping accounts and, perhaps even more important, no good system of auditing. Moor, when High Commissioner, handled what auditing system there was until after 1901, and thereafter it was the theoretical responsibility of the chief secretary.[35]

In 1912, Sir Frederick Lugard returned to Nigeria with

the new title of Governor-General, and a new task—to unite
Northern and Southern Nigeria. The immediate cause for amalgamation was economic, the same as that which dictated the
union of the southern areas in 1906. The northern protectorate,
landlocked and poor, was operating at a continual deficit. This
was met by a subsidy from the southern protectorate and grants-
in-aid from Britain.[36] By joining together the arid north with
the coastal south the British Government would be able to save
money and continue with development plans for the north envisioned by Lugard. It is somewhat strange, in retrospect, to
note that the Eastern Province continued to subsidize the North
after union while at the same time being almost ignored by the
central Government which favored the "more advanced"
north. A corollary economic reason for amalgamation was the
need to coordinate railroad policy. The southern line had
reached Jebba in 1909 and there were plans to continue it to
Minna. The northern government also planned to extend the
northern line to Baro, thus creating two competitive rail systems. In addition, work had begun on the eastern line which
was to pass through Enugu to the north. Amalgamation of the
Protectorate would solve the problem of coordination.[37]

Not all officials concerned with Nigeria agreed to unification. Lugard's lieutenant governor in the North wanted to break
up the great northern mass into seven separate provinces.[38] Lugard, however, had been given both the title of Governor-
General and special powers largely in order to bring about
amalgamation. His prestige was great and his closely reasoned
arguments difficult to refute, especially by men in the Colonial
Office with little knowledge of Nigeria. They ignored the recommendations of lesser men. Lugard's detailed proposal for
amalgamation was submitted to the Secretary of State on May
15, 1913. After a very brief scrutiny it was approved with few
changes and unification became reality on January 1, 1914.[39]

This amalgamation retained the divisions between North
and South with the exception that central offices such as Treasury, Military, Judiciary, and Railways were established. The
lieutenant governors of the North and South were in charge of
day-to-day administration with roughly the same freedom as

the previous Governors of the same areas. Only those problems that related to all of Nigeria were referred to the Governor-General, thus leaving him free to concentrate on continuous reform. The Legislative Council whose limited powers had been extended to all of Southern Nigeria in 1906, was confined to Lagos Colony only. In its place for the rest of Nigeria, Lugard established a Nigerian Council with a majority of official members. This unwieldy advisory body containing only six Africans could not act as a check on Lugard's policy.

Before amalgamation there were three provinces in the South. The provincial commissioner of each had powers which made him a *de facto* lieutenant governor. After creating the posts of lieutenant governor in the North and South, Lugard downgraded the provinces by splitting up the three into nine for the southern area. Each of the smaller provinces was in the charge of a resident who was directly responsible to the lieutenant governor. In the eastern section there were four provinces—Owerri, Calabar, Agoja, and Onitsha. Each of these provinces was then divided into three or more districts under the charge of a district officer aided by assistant district officers.

It is no exaggeration to say that Lugard was the architect of modern Nigeria. There were no checks on his power in Nigeria and except in a few instances, the Colonial Office gave him his head. The political structure of Nigeria, both in form and in spirit, which emerged after 1914 was highly favorable to the North because Lugard was biased toward that area. He made no serious attempt to understand the very complex traditional political structure of the East. With far less excuse than Moor or Egerton, he approached the problem of reform of the native-courts system, in the main, ignorant and unsympathetic toward these "backward" societies. As a matter of fact he dismissed Northcote Thomas, an anthropologist who had been employed by the Government of Southern Nigeria to study Eastern society. Lugard made it clear that he felt the best men to advise the Government on the nature of native society were not anthropologists, but good, dedicated political officers.[40]

As has already been indicated, there was an urgent need to revise the native-court system in the East. However, it is

F

doubtful whether Lugard could have improved upon Moor's creation even had he devoted more time to studying the East. Ignorance of existing situations was not the main impediment for Lugard. Rather it was his preconceptions which he rationalized and regarded as objective truth. Foremost of these was his conviction that his approach toward native rule in the North was correct and that with minor modifications it could be transferred to any section of Nigeria. Reinforcing this was the belief that it was imperative to develop a uniform system of native authority for all of Nigeria. The only way this latter objective could be attained was to assume that there were chiefs everywhere or, if they could not be found, that the society was backward and needed the stabilizing influence of appointed chiefs. Thus instead of questioning the first premise of the Native Courts Proclamations of 1900 through 1906, Lugard merely concenetrated upon what seemed to him the faulty details of those ordinances. Lugard's naïveté, not to say ignorance, of the situation in the East was betrayed in the following statement:

> At the time when Native Courts were first established in the old Southern Nigeria Protectorate, the *tribal authority*, had already broken down, and had been succeeded by a *complete collapse* of native rule under the *disintegrating* influence of middlemen traders and of the Aros. . . . The Native Courts no doubt did much to reestablish tribal authority and their usefulness is shown by their growing influence, and the number of cases with which they dealt. They had prepared the way for a further advance.[41]

The further advance was to be the Native Courts Ordinance of 1914 which attempted to establish a standard system of courts for all of Nigeria.[42] Four grades and five different courts were created. The "A" type of court consisted of either a paramount chief and his advisers or in the Muslim north an Alkali court. The B-, C-, and D-grade courts were those with varying jurisdictions operated by petty chiefs. Grade A courts never existed in the East. The highest-level courts there were the B grade which were the reconstituted Native Councils. The previous minor courts were to be mostly C grade, although the newly introduced D type was to be used for small areas and its jurisdiction was limited to debt cases not exceeding £10. The ordinance ended the Supreme Court's jurisdiction over Native Courts. After 1914 the realm of action of the Supreme Court was restricted to urban areas although Native Courts were still required to execute Supreme Court decisions and there could still be appeal through channels to the Supreme Court.

Lugard was opposed to European officers' sitting as ex officio presidents of Native Courts since he believed that this inhibited the development of a sense of responsibility by native members. Therefore, the ordinance restricted the political officers to a supervisory role, guiding the court until it became a true "native authority." The district officials, however, were not to interfere with proceedings unless gross injustice was being done. At any point, the district officer could transfer a case from a Native Court to his own.

A further ordinance created Provincial Courts with superior and concurrent jurisdiction to the Native Courts.[43] There was one court designated for each province where the resident acting alone could deal with civil cases up to £100 and could administer sentences up to five years' imprisonment and fines to a maximum of £100. District officers or assistant district officers could also act as a Provincial Court. In such a case they could handle civil cases up to £50 and give sentences of two years and levy fines to £50. A monthly list of all criminal cases was forwarded to the Governor-General and this served as an automatic appeal.

After his investigation of the previous native-court system, Chief Justice Osborne of Southern Nigeria had reported that "the dishonesty of the Native Court clerks was the chief evil of the system." [44] Lugard wanted to emphasize in the new regulations the fact that "the clerk is the servant not the master, of the Court." The Native Courts Proclamation attempted to check the excesses of the clerks by making them paid government servants rather than having them dependent on the revenues of their courts. It also attempted to simplify record keeping, requiring detailed reports to be kept only on land cases. The clerks in most cases, therefore, could keep only minimal records. No clerk was to be retained in one post for over two years. Lugard stressed that warrant chiefs were to keep a constant check on the clerks and to view them as the servants of the court and not superior to chiefs. Time would prove that these provisions did little to break the power of the clerks or to improve their honesty. Actually the provision that removed the district officers from direct participation in the courts gave the clerks even more opportunity to dominate the courts. The simplification of record keeping made it almost impossible in most cases for the political officers to reconstruct what had happened.

Two other "reforms" were to have similar detrimental effects on the courts. The position of traveling supervisor was abolished which removed another check on the actions of a corrupt court.[45] Lugard was also concerned that court messengers were being used to help maintain order and to arrest people. These were functions which only a chief should perform. Court messengers should be used only to carry messages. By restricting them to these duties the number of messengers could be reduced to only two or three for each court. Thus the warrant chiefs would be forced to perform their duties and would grow with the task. A further reason that influenced Lugard was that this reform would save money. Despite the protests of political officers, the number of messengers in the Eastern areas was drastically cut.[46]

It should be noted that from the time of the first Native Courts Ordinance there was in the East on the local level no separation of executive and judicial powers. The early proclamations issued by Lugard welded closer together these two functions. Despite this, Lugard wanted as soon as possible to separate Native Authorities from the Native Courts. Guided by the Northern model, he wanted to create effective chiefs in the East and eventually, perhaps, even paramount chiefs. In 1916 he instituted a Native Authority Ordinance and in the following year began to apply it in selected areas.[47] All residents were required to submit lists of chiefs who could be constituted "authorities." The reception of this by political officers in the Eastern areas was far from enthusiastic. Many protested that the act was premature and would result in a fragmentation of executive authority which would defeat the purpose of the legislation. In Calabar and Onitsha some chiefs were recommended and later 116 chiefs were selected for Calabar alone.[48] This type of approach, while being applied to coastal areas with minimal advantages, could obviously not be used in most of the East. As a result, by 1918 all the Native Courts in Owerri and Ogoja Provinces were constituted "native authorities."[49] This action effectively negated Lugard's wish to separate executive and judicial functions.

Many other schemes worked out by Lugard on paper were never put into effect in the East. One of these was to establish more courts with limited jurisdiction in order to cut down on the large numbers of court members.[50] This would also have helped to reduce the numbers of warrant chiefs in the East. However, such modifications would have called for almost a complete redesign of the system and therefore were never tried. Another plan was to establish special schools for the education of young men who would later become chiefs. Two major factors scuttled this plan. One was that political leadership did not necessarily pass from father to son so it was impossible to discover who would be the future chiefs. The second reason was that no suitable European could be found to head the school.[51]

When Lugard left Nigeria in 1919, he was convinced that he had put the native political system on the right road for further expansion and development. It was obvious that the redesigned native system had become even more institutionalized. A perceptive observer not tied to the establishment might have noticed that Lugard's careful creation in the East was a shambles. However, given the faulty first premises of most of Lugard's reforms, it is remarkable not that his plans did not work, but that they did not bring the entire prefabricated structure down about the heads of the British before 1929.

Lugard's successors, Sir Hugh Clifford and Sir Graeme Thomson, did not tamper with the basic structure created by their illustrious and influential predecessor. Their major concern with the Eastern provinces was to complete the task of bringing their political and economic practices into conformity with those of the rest of Nigeria. The central administration became increasingly concerned about the fact that Owerri, Calabar, Onitsha, Ogoja, and Warri provinces were not taxed. How could such a state of affairs be justified in the context of one Nigeria where presumably equal treatment was to be extended to all natives? The unique position of these provinces could not be tolerated much longer, but Clifford realized that the extension of taxation would have to be dealt with carefully. As one of the first steps in gathering the necessary information for this, Clifford sent S. M. Grier, the secretary for native affairs, to the Eastern provinces. Grier's report, submitted after an extensive two-month tour, was obviously a bombshell; not only did it advise against taxation, but it was brutally candid on the need to reform the entire structure of native administration.[52] He reported that even when traditional leaders were known to the British they were seldom on the Native Courts. Therefore, the prestige of the warrant chiefs was very low in the eyes of the people. Arguments for the popularity of the Native Courts based upon the number of cases heard were spurious since these were the only legal method of redress open to the people. The limits imposed by the Native Courts Proclamation also were responsible for the malfunctioning of the courts. Grier believed that throughout Iboland there were recognizable clan divisions but he found that only in rare instances did the native-court divisions follow these boundaries.

In 1914, Lugard and his advisers had been very critical of the court clerks and had been sure that the changes which they instituted would check most of the abuses. On the contrary, Grier found that removing the political officers from the Native Courts had left the courts at the mercy of these supposed functionaries. One political officer at Awka reported to Grier that he could spend his whole time investigating charges or bribery and corruption in the courts. If he did, 90 per cent of the warrant chiefs and clerks would be imprisoned.

Grier recommended a series of reforms, which were tantamount to scrapping Lugard's system, before taxation should be attempted. He suggested a careful mapping of the clan areas and a redrawing of the boundaries of Native Courts. Political officers should sit as presidents of Native Courts and take charge of all serious cases. Native clerks and messengers should be confined to their specific duties and strictly supervised. Wherever possible the hereditary leaders of towns and villages should be the only chiefs recognized by warrant. The old clan councils under clan chiefs should be revived and given limited jurisdiction over dowry cases, farm disputes, minor debt, and petty assault.

This negative report was not at all what Clifford expected. His only written comment on the report was an agreement that warrant chiefs should be, wherever possible, traditional leaders. However, he ordered no real investigation of Grier's charges and set down no guidelines for political officers to follow in determining the "real leaders." The only positive reaction of the Government was to send Grier's deputy, G. J. F. Tomlinson, to the Eastern provinces in 1923 to check on the veracity of the previous report. Obviously mindful of the reception of Grier's observations, Tomlinson was careful to stress in his conclusions that things were not too bad in the East and that Grier had been overly pessimistic.[53] A careful reading of Tomlinson's survey would have shown that, despite the conclusions, he agreed with Grier. This is most noticeable in a six-page analysis of "the Ibo Country." He began this by attempting to establish the criteria for judging the Native Courts when he wrote, "If, therefore, the Native Courts are to adapt themselves to a rapidly changing environment, it becomes necessary to enquire how far they may be said to be rooted in tribal institutions. So rooted, they will be capable of growth and adaptation. If not so rooted, they will sooner or later break down." [54]

In the survey which follows this statement Tomlinson shows that the Native Courts were not so rooted and that strenuous efforts would have to be made to appoint warrant chiefs who would be representative of traditional authority.

In the period prior to 1929 these warnings were echoed by many district officers. Practically every "reassessment report" after 1927 contained, on a more restricted level, information of the nonrepresentative nature of the Native Courts, their corruption, and the need for basic reforms.[55] It was the tragedy of Thomson's administration that these reports were ignored and that prior to the implementation of taxation little had been done to correct the most glaring deficiencies of the system. It was in this context of ignorance and complacency that Thomson decided to impose taxation on the Eastern provinces.

CHAPTER IV

The Decision to Tax

Extension of direct taxation to Southern Nigeria had occupied a prominent place in Governor Lugard's thoughts since early 1914. He believed that if Nigeria was to be truly united, the laws, political structures, and taxing procedures, should be as far as possible uniform in all parts of the territory. Dedicated to the concepts which he would later elaborate in his books and articles, he wanted to tidy up the lax government system of the Southern Provinces. One of the most glaring faults was the lack of direct taxation. It should be stressed that to Lugard, as well as his successors, Clifford and Thomson, added revenue was the least of the reasons for taxation. Lugard made this clear in his early communications on the subject with the Colonial Secretary, Lord Harcourt. He wrote that the establishment of a tax would not be "primarily due to a need of Revenue, but in order to enable me to set up a system of administration through the Native Chiefs somewhat on the model of the Northern Provinces." [1]

He elaborated on this further in another letter to the Colonial Secretary when he noted, "In my opinion the greatest value of a system of direct taxation is that it ensures the selection of the most capable and most influential men as the chiefs and advisers." [2] If indeed native treasuries were the foundations of self-government, then a scheme of taxation was necessary before African leaders could be educated in their responsibilities. Therefore, in August 1914, he requested of the Colonial Secretary permission to impose direct taxation on the South. Lugard wanted a similar carte blanche to that which he had been given in the North.[3] He proposed no detailed plans at this juncture and this obviously disturbed Lord Harcourt who refused the request. The Colonial Secretary, however, left the question open by inviting Lugard to forward more definite proposals if he wished. He warned the Governor to keep in mind the adverse effect upon Britain of a serious Colonial disturbance in time of war.[4]

In early 1915, Lugard sent H. Richmond Palmer on a tour of the Southern Provinces to sound out opinion relative to taxation. Palmer's report indicated that there would be little opposition by Africans except possibly in Lagos.[5] The Governor, after receiving this assurance, complied with Harcourt's request and communicated in detail his tax proposals. He divided the southern areas into three parts—based upon the degree to which chiefs and their councils exercised control. These were Yoruba-Bini, the eastern coastal provinces, and the eastern hinterland. Lugard wished to begin taxation in the first two areas since there was no danger of revolt there; the people were accustomed to strong rule by their chiefs and paying various kinds of tribute to their leaders. The administrative machinery was present and risks of the kind that disturbed the Colonial Secretary were minimal in these territories. Lugard made no proposal for the eastern hinterlands where these advantages were not present.[6] Despite such persuasive arguments, Lord Harcourt was still reluctant. The specter of a native rebellion made him warn again on the danger "however remote, of disaffection among the inhabitants of Nigeria" while the bulk of the armed forces were in the Cameroon.[7] He was also aware that the residents in the East were opposed to taxation. However, by 1916, Lugard had received permission to try his experi-

ment on a limited scale at Oyo. This proved so successful that
by the date of Lugard's departure all Southern territories west
of the Niger, with the exception of Warri, were paying a direct
tax.[8] The "no disturbance" dictum of the Colonial Office restrained the Governor from experimenting anywhere in the
east. However, the lieutenant governor of the Southern Provinces, A. G. Boyle, queried the residents in the east in 1918
concerning their attitudes toward taxation. Once again their
reports were negative and these helped to discourage Lugard
from pressing the Colonial Office further.[9]

The matter of extending taxation to the five provinces of
Warri, Ogoja, Onitsha, Owerri, and Calabar remained dormant
through the early years of Sir Hugh Clifford's administration.
Then in 1922, S. M. Grier, the secretary for native affairs, was
sent on a fact-finding mission to the East. As discussed previously, the main purpose of his two-month tour was to investigate the operations of the administrative and judicial system,
particularly among the Ibo. The bulk of Grier's extremely
critical report dealt with the malfunctioning of the warrant-
chief system.[10] Nevertheless, he did discuss taxation with the
residents and district officers and on the basis of these conversations Grier made a number of recommendations.

The opinion of the administrative officers was that taxation was much preferable to the system of unpaid labor provided for by the Roads and Rivers Ordinance. There were too
many abuses prevalent in the operation of this ordinance and
Grier recommended that when any tax scheme was applied to
the East the system of free labor should immediately be repealed.
Grier hedged the favorable opinion of the district officers
toward taxation with certain conditions that should be met.
The tax should be a capitation applicable to adult males, thus
avoiding the necessity of a complicated method of assessment.
More important, before any system of taxation was introduced
the shocking court system should first be reorganized. He reported that "all [the District Officers] are agreed that the collection of the tax can be left to the Chiefs." He advised that a
concerted attempt be made to discover the natural rulers of
the people and place them in positions of authority instead

of the Government-created warrant chiefs. Such a reorganization would take time and would need a full complement of administrative officers with experience of Eastern conditions. Perhaps most important, the central authorities would have to be willing to admit their past mistakes and, insofar as possible, correct them. The only comment which Governor Clifford made in his minute on the report was to agree that warrant chiefs without traditional authority should be removed. However, he noted that this would be a gradual process.

Grier's report was so critical of the system in the East that the assistant secretary for native affairs, G. J. F. Tomlinson, was sent to the same areas in January 1923. Tomlinson's investigation was a duplication of Grier's. He also spent two months in the East, mainly in Calabar and Owerri provinces. Tomlinson, despite his disagreements with Grier's harsh judgments of the political systems, agreed in almost every particular with the statements concerning taxation.[11] He believed it necessary to reestablish the native treasuries in order to facilitate self-government according to the Lugard concept. After 1914, all Native Court fees had gone into the general revenue and thus local officials had been deprived of the rights of managing their own money. Tomlinson wrote that taxation should be initiated in the coastal areas where native administration more closely paralleled traditional forms. It should then be gradually introduced in the hinterland. To accomplish this without difficulty, the Government should see that a full staff was provided for the Eastern areas and that the residents and district officers should be experienced men. The report laid emphasis on the need for a widespread and thorough introductory campaign before any tax scheme was implemented.

Tomlinson's report served to convince the central Government that Grier had overstated the corruption, inefficiency, and unpopularity of the warrant-chief system. As detailed elsewhere, little was done during the rest of Clifford's term of office to reform the government services in the East, which Grier had considered a necessary step before taxation could be safely introduced. Although taxation was not forgotten by Clifford's administration, nothing was done toward putting into effect any

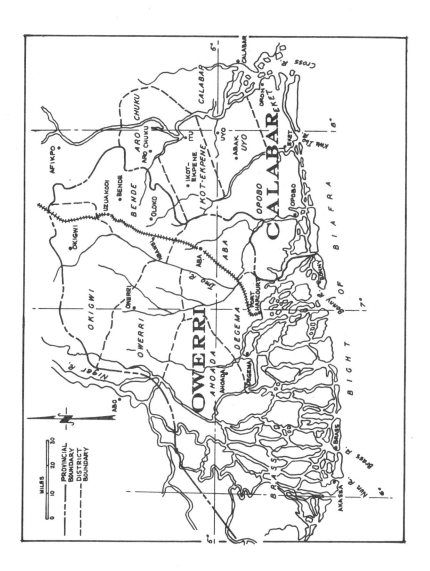

system in the East until August 1924, when Sir Harry Moorhouse, the lieutenant governor of the Southern Provinces, addressed a memorandum on the subject to the Governor.[12] Moorhouse traced the background of the tax question and pointed out the need to standardize policy throughout Nigeria. He suggested that it was time to bring the Eastern areas into line with the rest of the country. Sir Hugh decided that because of the short period remaining before the end of his term, he would not initiate any such radical program but would leave the decision to his successor.

A few days after his arrival, the new Governor, Sir Graeme Thomson, met with his closest advisers and the lieutenant governor of the Southern Provinces. In a minute dated November 17, 1924, the Governor agreed with Colonel Moorhouse's memorandum and gave his approval to taxing the five Eastern Provinces. He indicated that taxation should be introduced simultaneously in all the Eastern areas. Thomson requested the lieutenant governor to call on all residents to make reports and give suggestions concerning establishing the machinery of taxation for their provinces.[13] On December 2, the acting lieutenant governor, Captain Davidson, sent a circular containing basic information and instructions to the residents. Attached to the circular was a copy of Colonel Moorhouse's memorandum. A portion of the covering letter from the Secretary of the Southern Provinces related the forthcoming taxation to the Lugard philosophy, "I am also to refer you to Sir Frederick Lugard's Political Memoranda 5 and 9 which gave in general the principle on which taxation and Native Administrations are founded." [14]

The replies of the residents and district officers were guardedly pessimistic. None opposed the concept of taxation outright. However, their reports indicate the deep reservations which they held and which had not appeared in either Grier's or Tomlinson's report. A district officer in Owerri Province pointed out that it would be useless to consider any unit larger than the town for purposes of collection. He stated that a long period should be allotted for propaganda and assessment before the tax was instituted and suggested three years for such work.

The resident, Mr. F. B. Adams, while concurring in general, felt that the work could be completed in eighteen months.[15]

Mr. R. H. J. Sasse, the acting resident of Ogoja Province, reported that in his area the district courts could be used as the basic territorial unit. He concluded that all work of assessment and collection would have to be done by the European staff since there were no chiefs nor district heads of any recognized standing. He believed that the assessment register would take at least twelve months to complete.[16]

The gravest warning came from the resident of Warri Province, Mr. P. Amaury Talbot. He outlined some of the problems that might arise from trying to tax the independent but politically diffused Ibo and the unconquered Ijaws. Talbot expected physical assaults on the tax collectors and warned that the Government should be prepared to cope with this. For Warri he requested that the police force be augmented by one hundred men, one half of whom should be retained permanently.[17]

The lieutenant governor of the Southern Provinces, Major U. F. Ruxton, after receiving the comments of his administrative officers, worked throughout the summer of 1926 on a draft of a tax ordinance for the five provinces. At the outset he rejected the Native Revenue Ordinance of 1917 as not being applicable to the special problems of the East. He noted that "the basis on which the Native Revenue Ordinance rests in the Northern and Yoruba Provinces is completely absent so much so that its wording is unmeaning to officers in the Southern Provinces." [18] Ruxton proposed to keep the taxing procedure as simple as possible. He wanted a capitation on every male above the age of sixteen. Such a tax would eliminate the necessity of a long complex assessment program. It could be carried into effect by the administrative staff of the provinces with minimum difficulty. Ruxton, confronted with the complexity of native political forms in the East, made worse by the warrant-chief system, would have given to the residents the responsibility of collecting and disbursing the money. The tax would thus have been levied by the central Government and controlled by it. Ruxton's draft "general tax ordinance" was a very pragmatic measure, designed to meet the demands of a territory whose political institutions were unique in Nigeria.[19]

On September 15, 1926, Ruxton submitted a copy of the proposed ordinance to the lieutenant governor of the Northern Provinces, H. Richmond Palmer, for his comments. It should be noted that Palmer and the other main Northern commentator, C. W. Alexander, the resident at Kano, had had almost no experience with Southern Nigeria. They had spent the bulk of their careers in the North with its well-organized native political system. Except in some minority areas, they had never had to search for "natural rulers." These rulers had been apparent from the time Lugard first set foot in the North. It is, therefore, not surprising that the Northern officials were extremely critical of the draft.

Lieutenant Governor Palmer's main comments were that taxation should be based on a uniform theory throughout Nigeria, taxes should not be considered a direct Government levy, the main function of the bill should be to create viable systems of native rule (therefore the "chiefs" should be the main fulcrum of tax collection), and the residents should, as far as possible, confine themselves to an advisory role.[20] These arguments were echoed by Alexander from Kano.[21]

On November 5, G. J. F. Tomlinson, Secretary for Native Affairs, addressed a most important minute to the Government on the draft ordinance.[22] He stated that he was much impressed by the arguments of Palmer and Alexander and noted, "If I may say so, the Draft Ordinance seems to me to be far too literally *adapted to the facts as they exist today* and to contain insufficient provision for future development."[23] Further, Tomlinson wanted "to indulge in a little make believe" in reference to native treasuries' having collecting functions and make the treasuries an integral part of the scheme. That is, in theory if not in fact, they would have the taxes paid to them and they would then turn these over to the resident.

By November 1926, Ruxton's pragmatic approach had been all but destroyed by such arguments. Indeed, given the first premise on which the proposed taxation rested, it was inevitable that the theoretical approach should triumph. Ruxton himself recognized this when he had previously written,

> A curious paradox seems to arise from the fact that no manifest reason exists for now applying taxation to a people which, seemingly with intent, have never previously been taxed. During the war and later at times of considerable financial stress, direct taxation was not applied. It cannot today be said that new sources of taxation must be found in order to carry on; the only reasons that occur to me are almost ethical ones and therefore difficult to urge in Legislative Council.[24]

The truth was that Ruxton's draft, while a good compromise with reality, did not allow sufficient scope for the play of those "ethical" concepts. If the administration were to do the major share of the work, assume responsibility, and distribute funds, then taxation would not lead to the improvement in native administration envisioned by Lugard and his disciples. It would simply produce revenue.

Ruxton's draft ordinance for the five provinces was abandoned in November. Governor Thomson's note of the 18th indicated that the Native Revenue Ordinance would be amended to modify its complicated assessment provisions for the East.[25] This was to be done by inserting a new clause 6A, to the primary ordinance. The clause gave the Governor power by an Order in Council not to assess and collect in the manner prescribed by the ordinance but to levy a flat rate of ten shillings for all males over the age of sixteen.[26] Governor Thomson noted, "I desire, however, to make it clear that the new section [6A] is an instrument designed for temporary use only and that the method of assessment for which it provides will eventually be replaced by the more scientific method to which the advanced provinces have long been accustomed."[27]

Even this concession to the differences between the five provinces and the rest of the country was eventually dropped. After much debate the new clause 6A was deleted. On the

G

advice of the attorney general, Donald Kingdon, only one change was made in the 1917 ordinance. This was merely the insertion of a new Clause 2 of Section I to make the ordinance apply to all the Protectorate and not just to the Northern Provinces.[28] This change did not apply to the Colony which was to be covered by a separate income tax ordinance.[29] The Roads and Rivers Ordinance applying to the five provinces was also repealed as of April 1, 1928.

Taxation was to be introduced in the five provinces on April 1, 1928. Native treasuries were to be established in each province by October 1, 1927. In the interim six-month period, funds for these treasuries were to be derived from Native Court fees and fines. Instead of all these going to the general fund, 50 per cent would be retained in the provincial treasuries.[30] Another fateful a priori decision was taken by the Government in January 1927 in attempting the levy of a basic tax rate of seven shillings per adult male.[31] Thus, long before the district officers began their complicated task of finding the average earnings of men in their districts, Lagos had decided on a basic tax rate. This undoubtedly colored the report that the district officers submitted. Very few later disagreed with the recommended figure. The Government did not completely ignore the earlier comments of the residents and district officers. They had been warned to expect trouble when taxation was imposed on the East. Therefore, funds were voted to increase temporarily the number of police by five hundred rank and file.[32]

The proposed tax scheme, designed as a practical measure in the summer of 1926 by a man familiar with the peculiarities of the East, had become by January 1927 merely an extension of the Northern system to the five provinces. The criticisms made by Palmer, Alexander, and Tomlinson however unrealistic, were quite valid if one began with Lugard's premise that native treasuries were necessary for genuine local government to develop. The warnings of Grier and many residents and district officers had been ignored. The Native Courts and warrant chiefs were operating in 1927 as they had in 1924. Few changes had been made to rectify the most glaring errors in the native-court boundaries. To imagine that the warrant chiefs of the

East could function in the same manner as the emirs and chiefs in the North was to indulge in fantasy. The warrant chiefs were to prove a liability which the administration officers in the East were never able to overcome.

The Colonial Secretary Mr. Leopold Amery, questioned the advisability of extending the tax to all five areas at once, but gave Governor Thomson permission to do so if he liked.[33] Thus after more than two years of discussion, the Government had created the legal basis for taxation. It was now left to the men in the field to try to make the hypothetical structure work.

Administrative officers in the affected provinces were informed in November 1926 that a census of the population was soon to be taken in view of the imminent approach of taxation.[34] The form which the taxation would take was confirmed by the decisions of the central Government in the early months of 1927. On April the Chief Secretary's office announced the decision to start propaganda pursuant to the beginning of taxation.[35] The residents were to have the assessment reports completed and filed for further action before the end of the year. Although seven shillings had been established as the basic rate, district officers were not to consider this as a fixed figure. The actual rate should be calculated at 2.5 per cent of the average income of an adult male in each district.

This meant that district officers were confronted with a nearly impossible task. Their regular tasks were not to be neglected while the assessment was being done. In addition to their ordinary duties, the district officers had to make an accurate head count of the men in each village and to determine, with the cooperation of the warrant chiefs or traditional leaders, the number of men in each compound. An even more complex problem arose from the need to ascertain the economic wealth of each district so that the assessment rate would not fall beyond the ability of the "average" male to pay. While doing all this, they had to carry out a thorough propaganda campaign explaining the reasons for their activities and the advantages of taxation to people totally unaccustomed to paying any form of tax. In this propaganda campaign they had to obtain the support not only of the warrant chiefs, but also the long neglected "natural leaders" of the people. Instead of the three years suggested by the district officer of Owerri Province or even the twelve months asked for by the acting resident of Ogoja in 1926, the administrative officers were given approximately six months in which to do the necessary work.

In April 1927, the central Government sent Mr. W. E. Hunt on a tour of the affected provinces to help the administrative officers there in the propaganda campaigns.[36] He attended sixteen large meetings with chiefs and people from Ikot-Ekpene in the south to Nsukka in the north and Warri in the west. Most of his time was devoted to Owerri and Okigwi provinces. In all these meetings Hunt reported there was great hostility shown by the people to the idea of being taxed. Over and over he patiently explained the benefits that would accrue to them with the repeal of the Roads and Rivers Ordinance and their possession of native treasuries and eventual self-rule. The results of all this talk were largely negative as Hunt admitted when he wrote, "But for the most part my words were wasted, falling upon uninterested, uncomprehending or somnolent ears. Interest in benefits to come was swept aside by the thought of the imminent payment of money to the government." [37]

A general analysis of Hunt's report shows the attitude of the people throughout the area. At Ikot-Ekpene he was told that the people were too poor to pay and heads of families would have to sell their children to get funds. Similar comments were repeated at Itu, Aba, and Okigwi. He was asked at Itu whether the Government would prosecute the people if they sold their children. The proposed program was resisted by many of the warrant chiefs. Hunt was informed by the chiefs at Awgu that the district was so poor that it would be worth their lives to try to collect the tax. At Okigwi the chiefs were even more vociferous in their opposition. They said that they would be even more unpopular if they collected the tax. Therefore, they could not do so and would turn in their caps of office rather than try.

Despite all the evidence given him of the unpopularity of the tax measure in the areas he visited, Hunt remained very optimistic over the success of the program. He stated that the majority of the people were merely making a brave show of resistance to the inevitable. The people would accept taxation when it came with "fair grace."

No standard guidelines were established by the Government as to the method of assessment, propaganda, and eventual tax collection. Therefore, each district officer was free to institute the program he thought most effective for his area. The reports submitted by the officers were amazingly thorough, given the difficulties under which the writers operated. They were all aware of the complexity of the native society and a large portion of most reports was devoted to an analysis of the people in their district. It is obvious that a professional anthropologist would not have been satisfied with any of these reports. But the district officers were not trained in this discipline and were concerned primarily with the problem of taxation. Even had they been better trained, other factors mitigated against accuracy. As C. T. Mayne reported of the Umuahia court area in Owerri Province:

> The apathy and dislike of imparting knowledge of their tribal custom, life and origin was also unfortunately shared by the hereditary native head, who was almost always found to be the oldest man in the community, and therefore when seeking knowledge he was found adamant on every subject and the hope of obtaining reliable information faded.[38]

The most important fact emerging from these sketchy analyses of Ibo and Ibibio society is that the men in the field knew reasonably well the social and political bases of native society. K. A. B. Cochrane's report on Okigwi Division is perhaps the best of all the assessment reports in this respect.[39] His definitions of *family, compound, quarter, town, town group,* and *clan* were as good as those provided later by trained anthropologists. The district officers also knew who were the village headmen and town leaders and the fact that most of these held no legal authority. A. R. Whitman in reporting for the Elele District, Degema Division of Owerri Province wrote, "Instances have been put forward by the community for recognition by Government by the granting of a Court Warrant; it is still unfortunately the prevailing conviction that no man is recognized by Government as Head of a community unless he is created a Native Court Chief." [40]

Mr. G. E. Stockley, the assessing officer of Umuaturu court area in Degema Division, indicated his grasp of reality when he noted that many of the men indicated by warrant chiefs as headmen of villages were young. Since the head of a compound or of a village was usually old, Stockley noted that a given young man had been nominated "by the Warrant Chief as a suitable person through whom orders from the Government could be given to the people and he was not the real head of the compound as the people admitted on further questioning." [41]

Through these district officers' reports, the central Government was informed how shaky was the political structure which had been created in the East. The authorities responsible for introducing taxation were provided with specific illustrations of the truth of Grier's allegations made in 1922, yet they chose to ignore all these portents and no one seriously believed that taxation should be postponed until a major revision of the political structure was undertaken.

Some later commentators on the Women's Riots alleged that one of the reasons for these disturbances had been that the people in the East were not fully informed of the impending taxation in 1927. A careful reading of the assessment reports shows that this charge is not true. With only one exception, the assessing officers were at great pains to explain the reasons for their census and to convince the people that taxation would be preferable to their present condition. Captain A. Leeming's approach in Aba court area of Owerri Province can be taken as reasonably typical. In each of the ninety towns visited, he would hold general meetings with the people and there attempt to explain what the new taxes would mean in terms of benefit to them. He reported that he stressed the universality of direct taxes throughout the world and the fact that Britain "with the best civilization" was also the most heavily taxed.[42]

John Jackson in the Asa court area, Aba Division of Owerri Province, followed basically the same procedure and also held intimate conversations with the chiefs and elders, separate from those with the people. In these latter meetings he tried to convince the chiefs of the advantages to them of receiving salaries derived from tax funds. He pointed out that they would be consulted on estimates and the way the revenue would be spent. The people also would gain much directly by being paid for public works which they now were compelled to do for nothing.[43] F. J. Jenkins, the resident of Calabar Province, also printed fifteen hundred leaflets explaining the tax for distribution to the literate. He reported, "We could of course do with ten times that number, but funds for printing are not available." [44] By such activities the people of the East were made fully aware of the coming of taxation. The continual work regarding economic assessment and ultimately the instructions relating to collection amplified the earlier propaganda campaign.

The only area in which the assessing officer did not follow this pattern was in the Bende Division of Owerri Province. Faced with the known reluctance of the people to divulge information, the district officer did not inform the chiefs or people as to the purpose of the assessment. His method was to call upon the chief of a town before entering it. The chief was told to count the number of men, women, boys, and girls and to note their number on a paper. The district officer afterwards made a separate count and this was compared with the chief's figures and adjustments made. He stated, "The people were not aware that the counting had any connection with taxation and in this way a fairly accurate census of the Oloko and Ayaba Court areas were attained comparatively easily." [45] In March, however, as he stated, the Government released "the glorious tidings of the advent of taxation to an unappreciative Division." [46] Thereafter, matters became more difficult and it was decided to count the adult males only.

It is easy in retrospect to condemn the district officer for exceeding his instructions, particularly because this was the area where the women's disturbances began in 1929. A glance at the practical difficulties faced by the assessing officers in counting the men tends to moderate the judgment on this one official. One example of the problem can be seen in the report of John Jackson on the Asa Native Court.[47] There were twenty-eight villages in this area so his task was easier than in some of the larger districts. Nevertheless, he found it very difficult to arrive at an accurate count of the men, largely, he believed, because of the superstition about giving out the numbers of men, women, and children alive in the family. Such a recitation was supposed to bring misfortune or even death.[48] He noted further "It was not to be expected that the news of taxation would be received with unalloyed joy; it was on the other hand received with general sullen obstinate signs of defiance and refusal to accede to the demand." [49] The time was short; the complete survey of Asa was taken between May 4 and August 20, 1927. Therefore, Jackson modified his earlier attempts at a more accurate count and assumed one male for every three doors in the compound.

Similar accounts of difficulty are contained in every report and questionable assumptions made about the number of men in a village. In the Aba Division one method of arriving at the number of men in a compound was to assume three men for every eight rooms.[50] F. J. Jenkins, the resident of Calabar Province, wrote of his problems, "Information is refused, the people in most parts lock themselves up in their houses or desert their villages when an officer attempts to carry out assessment. The Chiefs decline to render assistance and give orders necessary to check this passive resistance." [51] He further warned, "It is clear to me that in some parts of this Province a few villages will have to be overawed by an armed force." [52]

The Government was prepared for sporadic outbreaks of violence in all sections of the affected provinces. Actual physical opposition to the assessment, however, was slight. Only in Warri Province was there a serious disturbance. This was the result of the fear that the Government planned to seize the land and the palm trees coupled with even more fantastic rumors that a man would be taxed three years after his death and all men and women would have to purchase licenses to live together. Led by the Sobo and Jekris people, the natives boycotted the Native Courts and refused to sell their palm produce. During the disturbances which lasted from August until the end of 1927, over two hundred police patrolled the area. The movement was eventually suppressed, however, with the loss of four lives.[53]

The threat of force by the Government in the other provinces served to block any serious resistance. An example of such a display of power occurred in Calabar Province where a chief informed the resident, E. M. Falk, that he was prepared to fight rather than cooperate. Falk accepted the challenge and sent the district officer, the assistant district officer, and twenty police constables to the chief's town within twenty-four hours. After seeing the town occupied so quickly by the police, the inhabitants bowed reluctantly to the inevitable.[54] Resistance to the initial taxation was certainly uniform in most of the East but it was a silent, nearly hopeless resistance.

In spite of the covert hostility by most of the people, the counting was accomplished in a very short time. Where it was not possible to make a direct head count, various approximations were used. A far more difficult task for the assessing officers was the estimation of the economic wealth of the "average" adult male. By adopting the complex assessing procedures used in the North, the administration forced the district officers to engage in complex, highly theoretical, and generally inaccurate estimates of the economic productivity of their areas. If the people had not been suspicious and in some cases hostile, a direct method of measuring sample farms, and questioning producers concerning yields and traders as to profits could have been used. Such a process would have allowed the district officers to arrive at reasonable estimates of the wealth of different villages. However, as previously noted, the people were "giving nothing away" and the assessors relied on a variety of highly questionable estimates.

In Okigwi District of Owerri Province, Cochrane arrived at the wealth of yam farmers by noting distances between yam hills and asking the farmers how many yams had been planted. He attempted to check this by an examination of the yam stacks of the previous year. In reporting this method he bluntly stated, "As far as possible I have avoided the actual measurement of farms for it would give the impression that a land tax was being imposed which is to be avoided at all costs." [55] In other areas such as Aba Division, the assessing officers did measure accurately some farms to arrive at what they considered an average farm holding. On a basis of the yields of yam, corn, and cassava from these samples they projected the earnings of all farmers in their division.[56] Similar methods were used in Bende and Degema Divisions.[57] The count of oil palm trees was also hampered by fear of arousing false suspicions of the aim of the census. It was therefore necessary to estimate the number of trees controlled by the "average" farmer and the yearly yield from these trees.

Once theoretical figures of productivity had been established, the assessing officers then had to convert these to monetary terms. They accomplished this by establishing the current market price of each item and multiplying the figure by the average yields to each male farmer. Their task here was made easier because almost all the men in the village were engaged in farming. They did not have to consider any other trade or profession.

The short time given to the district officers to complete their reports and the hostility of the populace precluded any detailed breakdown of the adults actually engaged in profitable farming. Thus the annual income reconstructed by the questionable methods was assumed to be the same for all adult males. Most district officers were aware of the inequity. C. T. Mayne of Bende Division noted in his report that men under the age of nineteen would also be assessed and that in almost every case they had no land, livestock, nor trees. The young men normally lived in the father's or a relative's compounds and these older men would thus be required to pay a double tax.[58]

Another inequity in the assessing practice was to make no distinction between products harvested specifically for marketing such as oil products and those which would be used for family consumption. A large portion of the yam and cocoa yam harvest was never sold but was used for food. In some areas livestock was also considered on a basis of their market value even though the goats and sheep were seldom sold. Since the initial assessment was to be used for taxing purposes for a number of years, the figures for livestock evaluation would be valid only if there were a 100 per cent yearly increase. The reality of the assessment was to measure not an individual's annual earning capacity, but his total wealth, discounting only possessions such as buildings, furniture, and utensils.

Except in very poor areas such as Isu and Ochi in Okigwi District and the Ebem court area of Bende Division, the reports are fairly uniform as to the taxable income of adult males. The figures given varied roughly between £12 and £14 per year. Only in Elele Province of Degema Division were the figures reported so high as to be obviously wrong.[59] The assessing officer there estimated that the annual income of a married family head was £64. The resident of Owerri Province, O. W. Firth, in a covering letter declared that this was patently erroneous. He recommended that the tax rate for this area should be set not at 2.5 per cent of £64, but at a flat seven shillings per male. Even this magnanimous gesture illustrated how faulty the system was. The district officer had spent months arriving at his inflated figure only to have the resident disregard his report and arbitrarily suggest a tax rate. Firth acted in the same manner with regard to other districts where he felt the recommended tax rate was too low.[60]

Many of the district officers not only noted the problems of assessment but also indicated their appreciation of the people's viewpoint. Mayne in Bende Division expressed this best when he wrote, "I am much in sympathy with the natives, especially those in the more remote parts of the area, who in my opinion, will gain little or no material benefit from the imposition of the tax although they have been continually told the advantages they will be gaining!"[61]

Another assistant district officer of Bende echoed this feeling and warned that if there were not immediate tangible results such as the beginning of a road it would be almost impossible to collect the tax in 1929.[62]

Despite the many problems which confronted the administrative officers, all the assessment reports with the exception of those from Warri had been received by Lieutenant Governor Ruxton in December 1927.[63] The tax schedule for the five provinces was established early in 1928. In the two provinces which would later be the scene of the women's protest, Owerri and Calabar, the basic rate suggested before assessment was changed in only a few instances. In Calabar Province the Ekoi area was assessed at five shillings and Opobo at eight shillings. In all other districts the rate was seven shillings. In Owerri Province the standard rate was seven shillings per adult male with the exception of Okigwi and Orlu districts at six shillings and Bende District with a few exceptions at a low five shillings. The Lieutenant Governor stated that these rates were reasonable and well within the range of the people's income.[64]

Collection of the tax began almost immediately after the ordinance came into effect in April 1928, and was almost complete by the end of June. Methods of collection varied from district to district. Native Court areas were used as the administrative center for gathering taxes from the villages. In some places the warrant chiefs acted under the administrative officers as the chief collectors. In other districts the villages paid the tax money directly to the district officer. The usual procedure, however, was to utilize the traditional village heads to collect the rates from their people. They would be given papers on which had been noted the amount to be collected from each compound. After this had been done the money was turned over to the administrative officer who checked to see that all who were required to do so had paid the tax. This method was a direct refutation of the system of native administration built up by previous governors and maintained under Thomson. In the past the traditional heads had been all but ignored by the central government which was convinced that the warrant-chief system, at the very least, represented a real compromise with the old, unmanageable local government. In order to assess and collect the new tax adequately, the British discovered that they had to depend not on their creations, the warrant chiefs, but on the neglected village elders.

Notwithstanding the difficulties and the threat of non-cooperation and even violence by the natives, the tax collecting in 1928 proceeded smoothly. There were only a few disturbances in all the five provinces, most of these being confined to

Ogoja and Onitsha provinces. In the former area the Ezza and Ezzi subtribes refused to pay. Administrative officers toured both areas discussing, cajoling, and threatening the people. This was enough to bring the Ezza into line. However, the Ezzi remained adamant in their refusal. Many village meetings were broken up by crowds of women who mobbed the older men when they showed signs of agreeing to the tax. This was the first indication of active interference against taxation by women in any of the Eastern Provinces. Police were sent to the Ezzi area and a number of the women leaders were arrested and tried in the Native Courts. The agitation against the tax then soon died out.[65]

Opposition to the new system was also noticeable among the Ekumuru and Assiga tribes in Obubra Division of Ogoja Province. This too faded away without harm being done. In the Awgu Division and the Achi Native Court Area of Onitsha Province there were boycotts against the tax as well as the Native Courts. The ringleaders of the protest were arrested and tried, and the overt opposition ceased.[66] In Owerri Province, native treasuries came into being on October 1, 1927, and there were no reports of extraordinary resistance to the collection of the tax in the entire province. Calabar, the other province which would be deeply disturbed by the riots in 1929, also presented no difficulties during the initial collection period.

The central authorities had every right to be pleased with the implementation of the ordinance. The dire predictions of such experts as Resident Jenkins of Calabar Province had not proved correct. Despite the obvious reluctance of the people to pay, they had caused very little trouble. At the close of the fiscal year, £364,824 had been collected. Of this sum, 50 per cent was usually retained by the native administrations. In the case of a few "fully organized" administrations, the proportion retained was 70 per cent.[67] The construction of new native administration offices and council houses financed by the taxes was begun throughout the Eastern Region. The satisfaction felt after the first year's tax was confirmed by the experiences of the second year when even less opposition was encountered and the total return was £324,690.[68]

The authorities were not complacent for there was still much to be done. In most districts the village census rolls were not accurate and these would have to be revised. Something also had to be done to bring the people into more direct contact with planning the estimates and spending the local tax funds since there was normally only one treasury for an entire district. To achieve Lugard's concept of the natives' learning correct government practices by spending their own funds, the district officers would have to find ways of relinquishing some of their control of these funds. The assessment and taxation had shown how inadequate the warrant chiefs were. The policy announced as early as Clifford's administration of phasing out the government chiefs who did not have the respect of their people should be implemented as quickly as possible without totally upsetting local government. Also native-court boundaries in many cases needed to be rectified. But this, too, would take time and there was no need to rush into anything. Taxation had been accepted by the people in the East with less disturbance than had been expected. The special police force of five hundred which had been raised in 1928 to cope with resistance was reduced. Some of the rank and file were absorbed into the regular force, but most were released. The total number in the special force in December 1929 stood at 183 of which forty-four were in Calabar Province and only nineteen in Owerri.[69]

The closing months of 1929 saw a self-satisfied government, convinced that their policies had been accepted in the East. The whirlwind that would shatter this complacency and destroy the carefully wrought, theoretical government came from a totally unexpected quarter. The women of Owerri and Calabar provinces, not cowed by the presence of British power, pushed against the structure and in a short time brought it down.

CHAPTER V

The Beginning of
the Disturbances

Ibo and Ibibio society in the 1920's was subjected to a series of pressures, most of which were not discernible to the administration. The old order was changing rapidly under the impact of Western religion, economics, and the synthetic political structure maintained by the British. It is probable that had there been no taxation in the East there would have been, in time, disturbances caused partly by the schisms between the new and the old within native society. The imposition of taxes merely served as the focal point for a whole series of dissatisfactions inherent within the society.

In assessing the background of the disturbances of 1929, one must be careful in assigning weight to the various forces that contributed to the unrest. Even from a vantage point of almost forty years, it is impossible to give definitive answers as to what actually caused the sudden explosion against British rule. It is doubtful whether even the leaders of the women knew what impelled them toward revolt. The answers that they gave to the commissions of inquiry indicated that they were motivated by short-range goals and impelled largely by emotion.

The attempted reconstruction of the causal factors by administrative officers after the event is in some ways more satisfactory. However, these explorations were written by men outside the society and, however logical they may seem, are really speculative to a large extent. Thus, one is left with a hard core of obvious political, social, and economic reasons for the disturbances and still it is not possible to assign priorities to the reasons for the reaction in any specific area. The narrative of causes which will be attempted here should be considered descriptive and speculative and definitely nondogmatic.

Economic factors seem to be the most important in causing the disturbances of 1929. As outlined in the previous chapter, the scheme of taxation which was completely foreign to the people was imposed in a hurried and nondiscriminating fashion. Young men who had no real earning power were taxed the same as responsible older men. The women were also affected. Although there was a division between the men's income and that of the women of a compound, it was not rigid. Husbands were supposed to provide money for certain things, particularly luxury items for special occasions. In some of the poorer households the tax reduced the man's ability to provide these. In many cases also the women had to resort to their savings to provide tax money for their men. The intertwined nature of the village economy was such that the initial assessment had been based not only upon the man's wealth, but also upon items which had traditionally been considered to belong to women.

Women in the Eastern Region were deeply involved in trading. Some conducted their small trade only in the local markets, but others were involved in more important transactions in the larger markets such as Aba or Calabar. In many cases they acted as intermediaries in providing the European firms with palm oil and palm kernels. They also conducted trade in imported items such as cloth, tobacco, cigarettes, and spirits. Any alteration in the selling price of oil or in import duties would therefore affect the women as much as the men.

From 1922 through 1928 the price of palm products had been slowly but steadily improving. However, in 1929 the first tremors of the worldwide depression reached Eastern Nigeria and the prices received by traders in all areas were appreciably lower than in previous years. The following table of prices paid for palm products at various markets gives an indication of how serious this loss of money was: [1]

| | PRICE OF 4 GAL. OIL | | PRICE OF 50 LB. KERNELS | |
PLACE	DEC. 1928	DEC. 1929	DEC. 1928	DEC. 1929
Aba	5/9	4/6	7/0	5/10
Oguta	6/6	5/6	5/9	5/-
Owerri	5/6	5/6	4/6	3/9
Okpala	7/-	5/6	5/9	4/-
Ngor	6/6	5/-	4/6	3/9

In most of the towns of Owerri and Calabar provinces the traders suffered 8-12 per cent loss in their earning capacity in a twelve-month period.

In 1929, produce houses were changing their method of purchase from buying by measure to buying by weight. This system was being newly introduced in Owerri Province, but in Calabar, with the exception of Opobo, it had become the practice.[2] The change, combined with the lower prices paid, convinced some women that they were being cheated. The Government contributed to this unrest by instituting a program of inspection of produce.[3] It is impossible to say what effect this had on the traders, but it was another instance of Government interference in a market that was just beginning to fail.

In February 1928, the Government introduced a new scale of duties which it believed would help ease the cost of living for the natives since it abolished the 15 per cent duty on imported food. In reality this provision affected the people very little since, with the exception of stockfish, they purchased little imported food. On the other hand, the provisions of the act which raised the duties on "luxury" items did terrific damage to the traders. Import duties on tobacco were raised from one shilling, six pence to two shillings per pound, on cigarettes from one shilling, six pence to two shillings per hundred, and on

H

spirits from twenty-five shillings to twenty-seven shillings, six pence per gallon.[4] These items were the main trade goods of many market women and the higher duties combined with the factors which reduced their capital usually meant a substantial loss in profits.

Women traders were in no position to analyze these events philosophically. They could only observe that within a year certain factors had combined to reduce the amount of money that they had. Taxation, lower prices for raw materials, higher prices for luxury items, and new rules for selling produce could all be viewed as stemming from a conspiracy of the Europeans to impoverish them.

Before attempting to deal with the beginnings of the women's protests one must investigate further the role of women in the East, particularly in Calabar and Owerri provinces. As noted previously, while there are many differences between Ibo and Ibibio organization of society, there are also fundamental similarities. In each of these, women traditionally exercised more influence than was typical in an African society. In addition to their influential role as wives and mothers, they were accustomed to being consulted on issues affecting the village. Although they could not own land, there were many ways by which they could lease or use it. Surplus food for which they were responsible, such as cocoa yam and cassava, could be sold and they could retain the proceeds. They were directly involved in the palm oil trade, some of them becoming extremely wealthy, and the bulk of the petty trading was in their hands. Their work as traders took them beyond the narrow confines of their own villages and this combined with exogamy gave the women of one village the ability to influence other women over a wide area.[5]

In traditional village life Ibibio and Ibo women participated directly in a number of organizations; some of these regulated only women's affairs, but there were some that could influence decisions usually reserved for men among most African groups. Among the Ibibio the women had their own well-organized society which took its name (*Ebre*) from the annual celebration of the harvest of the women's yams. The society was open to women of all ages and acted as both a social and policing agency. The society carried out the many ceremonies directly related to women, supervised their actions and punished them for breaking any of the rules of the society. The existence of village Ebre societies throughout the Ibibio areas meant a generalized acceptance of certain values and provided a base for common action against the authorities in Calabar Province.[6]

There was a greater variation of social and political forms among the Ibo and therefore it is more difficult to isolate standard women's institutions through which protest could be channeled. In some Ibo areas, notably in Owerri Province, there was a women's society called *Eyoro*.[7] It seems to have been roughly comparable to the Ibibio Ebre society. However, it existed in no more than a few villages. In areas where the *ozo* title was prevalent, women could also, in theory, take the title although the initiation ceremonies were different from those of the men. A woman who had taken such a title was referred to as a *Lolo*.[8] The practice of women's assuming the ozo privilege does not appear to have been common. Perhaps the most common organization among most of the Ibo groups was the *mikiri* (*mitiri*) type of association.[9] Rules governing a mikiri varied from one area to another. In some places it was reserved exclusively for women while in others men could also belong to it. A village mikiri that met at regular intervals performed a number of functions. It acted as a means of bringing people together to sing, dance, and talk. Money was collected from the members to pay the costs of the meetings, the surplus in any instance being retained by the person who had been responsible for providing the food for that meeting. Members of a mikiri also established standards of behavior for their group and could punish those who broke the rules. A common requirement for exclusively women's mikiris was that the members had to be born in the village. This meant that women who, owing to the practice of exogamy, became permanent residents in their husband's villages would return to their home villages for the mikiri meetings. Thus in any meeting women from a dozen or more villages would be brought together and news and grievances could be shared.

Captain J. N. Hill, District Officer at Bende, reported the existence of an "Ogbo" society which he believed to have functioned throughout Owerri Province prior to the disturbances.[10] Its organization had predated the coming of British rule and it was open only to women. The society was presumably democratic as the leaders were selected by vote and their position within the society did not depend upon their husbands' status. The major function of the society was a social one, but it could also bring the full weight of its membership to support the cause of anyone who belonged to it. According to Hill's report, the societies were grouped into areas roughly conforming to the Native Courts. Each town would take its turn as the meeting place for the society in the court area. When matters of importance arose, the women of all the towns in a locality would meet and pass information on to the next area. Thus the action taken by one local Ogbo society on a specific matter could be transmitted throughout the country in a very short time. The secretary of the Southern Provinces, C. T. Lawrence, writing in 1930, was convinced that this society provided the philosophy and machinery for the women's disturbances.[11]

If the Ogbo society did exist it was certainly in a form different from that described by the British administrators. In all the literature related to Ibo culture, there is no mention of such a well-organized, all-pervasive society. It seems probable that Hill had been informed of the mikiri and assumed that it was similar in its structure to the Ibibio Ebre society. However faulty the British understanding of the details of the women's organization, their conclusions were basically correct. Women meeting together at the markets and more formally at mikiris could share their fears and grievances. In the tense atmosphere of 1929, the details of alleged wrongs to one village could become, within a short period of time, common knowledge to women throughout a province. Plans for action to be initiated against authorities in one village could rapidly become the basis for similar protests in most of the Eastern areas.

The widespread dissatisfaction with the corruption and inequities of the warrant-chief system, therefore, was not confined to the men. The women, with a long tradition of freedom and participation in political affairs, with their business interests, and with such potentially powerful organizations, were in the forefront of the protests against the political system. With the advent of taxation of the men and the beginnings of economic depression it would have been surprising if the women had not been active.

In the testimony given before the commissions of inquiry, one theme occurred again and again. This was perhaps best expressed by Chief Akpan Udo Lekpo of Calabar Province when he said of the riots, "I never saw the women carrying on in this fashion before. I never before this time saw the women flinging sand at their chiefs and white men and attacking them with sticks." [12]

Perhaps he and the other chiefs who agreed with him had never witnessed such a furious reaction by the women, but there had been other violent protests by them in the four years preceding the uprising. The first of these occurred in Calabar town on April 1, 1925, and was caused by the imposition of The Ibibio and Efik women refused to pay them since they had tolls, under the Market Ordinance, to the two Calabar markets.[13] not been consulted nor had the rules ever been explained to them. Rumors had been circulated that any woman who wanted to go to the market would be charged a penny and this rate would also be charged for use of the public latrine.

Trouble began without warning when the women drove off laborers who were building a fence around Marina market. The disturbance spread to Bush market where the women swarmed through Government Gardens to invade Government Hill. By ten o'clock in the morning, the crowd there had grown to approximately three thousand women and the commissioner of police read the Riot Act. By this time all factories on the river front were closed. The women assaulted Europeans, native foreigners, and the police. After an hour of this the police were ordered to drive the women back by using their rifle butts. The Marina was cleared, guards were stationed at the factories, and there was no more violence. However, before the situation returned to normal, the women closed the markets and tried to impose fines upon anyone who sold food to Europeans.

A smaller protest movement of approximately two hundred women occurred at Oton a few days later but the resident was able to convince them that no tolls would be imposed on their market.

Another protest by women occurred in November 1925 and was called the Dancing Women's Movement. It first affected Okigwi Division of Owerri Province.[14] The reason for the movement was supposed to be a miraculous truth which had first been revealed by God to the people of Bonny and Degema and then had spread northward. The exact nature of this truth was never revealed to Europeans, but the women considered it a sacred duty to spread the good news. Bands of women went from town to town and made demands on the people and, by implication, on the Government. At first these demands appeared reasonable—for example, better sanitation, increased childbearing (the meaning of this demand was never clarified), a return to the old customs, and closer regulation of prostitution. However, as the movement spread new demands were added, many of which concerned the economic and political system. Among other things, they wished prices of foodstuffs in the markets to be fixed, and in some places they wanted a ban on using European coins and a return to brass rods and manillas.

The women's activities were particularly strong at Umuahia in Bende Division and also at Awgu. Here the story was circulated that all Europeans were leaving and that no more government work was to be done—therefore the Native Courts should be abolished. At Iboko in Abakaliki, threats of burning the Court and rest houses were made, and at Isu this was actually done. In some places bands of women threw sticks and stones at automobiles. Troops were finally sent into the affected areas and order was restored by the end of December 1925.

Another disturbance with totally different objectives but similar methods was the Spirit Movement which began in 1927.[15] These general disorders among the Ibibio in Calabar Province also caught the authorities unaware. It began in the Kwa Ibo Mission in Uyo District and was ostensibly Christian oriented. Persons possessed by the Spirit exhibited such symptoms as foaming at the mouth, rolling their eyes wildly, and contorting their limbs. The leaders demanded that all people should publicly confess their sins. The authorities first took note when an hysterical band in Ikot-Ekpene broke up objects sacred to the "pagan" people of the area. Unlike the Dancing Women's Movement, both sexes participated in the Spirit Movement, but it was observed that women made up the largest portion of the bands. Before spreading to Itu several murders were committed in the vicinity of Ikot-Ekpene and large numbers of police had to be brought in before the area was calmed.

At Itu, gangs inspired by the Spirit lived in churches and preyed upon those who resisted them. Their main targets were the non-Christian elements in the population, especially chiefs or their families. Those who refused the invitation to publicly confess their sins were seized and tortured. One of the favorite methods was to bind people up, using levers to tighten the thongs. Then they would pour water on the victims and leave them to die. A detachment of police rushed to Itu and were in time to save twenty-nine people who had already been trussed up, although five people had previously been killed. Once the Government committed the police, the entire movement faded away.

The Spirit Movement at first was allied with Christianity and led by the younger converts. Soon it degenerated into a search for witches with many of the adherents falling back on the catharsis of the old Ekpe and Idiong secret societies. The movement affected the lower orders of society and was directed primarily against the chiefs and elders who took no part in it and tried to suppress it. It constituted a revolt against organized authority and women played a most important role in the disturbances.

Reference has already been made to the action of the Ezzi women in Ogoja Province who in 1928 repeatedly broke up meetings composed of men who might favor the Government plan of taxation. Their activities were brought to an end only by the arrest, trial, and conviction of their leaders.[16]

As different as each of these movements seemed to be, they had a number of things in common. First there were real problems and grievances at the root of each disturbance. They all surprised the authorities since there was no warning of the women's plans. The movement or the reports of the activities of the women traveled rapidly. In some cases swift action by the police kept the protests confined. In others, such as that of the Dancing Women, even the quick response by the Government did not check it until it had affected an entire province. Thus if the authorities in the autumn of 1929 had looked carefully into recent history they could have seen how the women had come together in a concerted, violent, antiauthoritarian protest against policies far less detrimental to them than taxation. The administration in the Eastern Region was certain, however, that the worst of the protests against taxation had ended. The people had paid their taxes, unwillingly perhaps, for the previous two years. Warrant chiefs and the traditional rulers had learned the danger of openly opposing the British power. Complacency prevailed from the chief secretary's office down to the cadets serving as assistant district officers. It should also be noted that the administrative establishment in the five provinces was under strength. Many of the assistant district officers had had little experience and the police force, concentrated largely in Calabar, was not strong enough to respond to challenges throughout the Eastern Region.[17]

The spark that ignited the conflagration in the East was supplied by a young assistant district officer in Bende Division of Owerri Province. This was the same division where in early 1927 District Officer A. L. Weir had deceived the people as to the purpose of the initial tax census. Only when his hand had been forced by actions of the central Government had he informed the chiefs and people that the men were going to be taxed.[18] In September 1929, Weir, who was going on leave, turned over the administration of the division to Captain John Cook who would be in charge until the new divisional head, Captain Hill, arrived in November.[19]

The census registers for the division were inaccurate and incomplete. It was standing policy that administrative officers, in their spare time, should attempt to revise the initial counts. No pressure was exerted by the resident or higher officials to correct or modify the registers and certainly no deadline established for the filing of new reports. The central Government was satisfied with the established tax rate and the collection. In October, however, Cook on his own authority decided to establish nominal rolls and to obtain accurate information on the number of men, women, children, and livestock. The new count was to be introduced first in the Oloko Native Court Area.

Cook held a meeting with a few of the chiefs in Oloko on October 14 and told them the reason for the new census. They were informed that this had nothing to do with changing the tax system and that the Government did not contemplate taxing the women who were to be counted. Despite this assurance, a number of warrant chiefs later called meetings of the elders of villages and told them that the new count was for the purpose of taxing the women and levying duties on livestock. When these elders returned to their villages, they told their wives. Within hours the news had spread over all the Oloko area. In the following week the women held village meetings at Umuosu, Mbwpongo, and elsewhere in the court area. Leaders of the women in Oloko called a general meeting of women at the Orie market.[20] Before this meeting convened, women from villages outside Oloko had talked with their chiefs and had also been told that the new count was preliminary to taxing them.

Warrant Chief Okugo at Oloko was an elderly man who was considered by the administration to be a weak and ineffective leader. However true this might have been, he was intelligent enough to know the hazard of attempting a census in the face of the women's opposition. Later charges made against him, that he had misinformed the women, were negated by other testimony during the investigation by the Commission of Inquiry. His actions also belied the charge that he had told the women they were to be taxed. Okugo's instincts for holding on to his position told him to do nothing. He followed this policy even after other chiefs had begun to prepare for the census. On November 18, Captain Cook berated him for his slowness and ordered him to have the counting in Oloko finished in

eight days. Even then the prudent Okugo employed someone
else to take charge of the census. The unhappy task fell to an
unemployed schoolteacher named Mark Emeruwa who viewed
the census merely as another job to be done and immediately
began the count.

The meeting of the women at the Orie market established
the line of action which the women would take. It also brought
out how well disciplined the women were. The leaders in the
Oloko Native Court Area were three women, Ikonnia, Nwannedie, and Nwugo, who in the coming weeks displayed their
political sagacity and at the same time rigidly controlled the
activities of the other women. It was decided at Orie that the
women should wait to see definite signs that they were to be
taxed before acting. As long as the assessors approached only
the men in a compound, seeking information, the women
should do nothing. However, if any woman were approached
directly and asked to give the number of women and livestock
in her house she was to raise an alarm and call the other women.
They would then decide what to do.

Assessor Emeruwa seems to have been very scrupulous in
his approach to counting in the different compounds. All questions concerning the numbers of people or animals would be
directed toward the man who was head of the household. Thus
until November 23, the women had no evidence that they were
going to be taxed. On that day Emeruwa went to the compound of a man named Ojim and asked to speak to him. What
actually occurred between Emeruwa and Nwanyeruwa, Ojim's
wife, will probably never be known since their testimony was so
much in conflict. Nwanyeruwa claimed that he began to ask
her questions concerning the people in the compound. Harsh
words were obviously exchanged and there was a scuffle between
the two. Emeruwa maintained that the woman had insulted and
then attacked him. Nwanyeruwa claimed that Emeruwa became enraged at what she said and tried to choke her. Whatever
the truth of the affair it provided the proof that the women of
Oloko were waiting for.

Emeruwa immediately complained to Chief Okugo who
sent for the woman and threatened to report her actions to the

district officer. After leaving the chief's compound Nwanyeruwa proceeded directly to a meeting of the women which had been scheduled earlier. Nwanyeruwa related to the Oloko women her version of what had happened. This convinced the women that they were going to be taxed and they decided to resist. Palm leaves, a signal of distress, were sent out to neighboring areas and the messengers were instructed to ask all women to come to Oloko to protest against taxation there and make plans for opposition to the tax elsewhere. The response to the Oloko women's request was immediate and in the next few days women streamed into Oloko from all over Owerri Province. Representatives from as far away as Aba, Owerri, and Ikot-Ekpene arrived to take part in the discussions and demonstrations.

On the evening of November 24, the women of Oloko camped in front of Emeruwa's compound at the Niger Delta Pastorate Mission and "sat on him." That is, they sang, danced, and drank palm wine to keep him from sleeping and prevent him from doing his ordinary tasks. The next day large numbers of women besieged Chief Okugo in his house. He set his retainers on them and they were driven away. Okugo then sent a plea for help to the district officer at Bende. The women also sent a deputation to Bende to report on Okugo's alleged cruel actions. On the 26th the women returned to Okugo's house in great numbers and this time they demanded his cap of office. His servants could not drive them away this time. The women pressed forward threateningly and Okugo escaped to take refuge in the Native Court compound.

The following day Captain Cook arrived from Bende, accompanied by four police, and found approximately a thousand women waiting for him in the marketplace. At first he could learn nothing from the women, but later a deputation informed him of their fears of being taxed and their version of the events that had taken place after November 23. Cook told them that the Government had no intention of taxing them and later put this assurance in writing for the leaders. This satisfied the women but they now demanded that Chief Okugo be released to them. On Cook's refusal most of the crowd, by then grown to approximately twenty-five hundred, dispersed. However, they were back the next day, this time with women who claimed to have been injured by the chief and his servants. The women wanted Okugo to be arrested and immediately tried. Cook informed them that he could not try Okugo since he was going to hand over his office to the new district officer, Captain Hill. Nevertheless he did arrest Okugo, charged him with assault, and took him to Bende on November 29.

The removal of Okugo did not end the affair since the women's leaders had resolved to see the chief punished. Cook, whose actions had initiated the disturbance, handed over his authority to Captain Hill on November 30 and left Bende on Monday, December 2. Hill, inheriting a situation not of his own making, was alarmed at the number of women flooding into the town. His position was extremely weak yet he hesitated to telegraph for police reinforcements. On the day that Cook left for Enugu, Hill found himself confronting an estimated ten thousand women gathered about the Government offices. At this time they seemed to have been reassured that they would not be taxed. What they now wanted was Okugo to be handed over to them. Failing this they wanted an immediate trial. When Hill informed them that the trial could not begin before Thursday, the women made a rush for the offices. Without sufficient police, Hill then committed a major, if understandable, blunder. As he stated later, "They demanded his [Okugo's] Cap of Office which I threw to them and it met the same fate as a fox's carcase thrown to a pack of hounds." [21]

Obviously Captain Hill's memory was as faulty as his judgment. His testimony before the Commission of Inquiry would indicate that he was dealing with a bloodthirsty, undisciplined mob which, in lieu of the body of Okugo, joyfully dismembered his cap. It is, therefore, difficult to explain how this same cap was later returned to the district offices untorn and in good condition.[22] This small detail is important in creating doubt about the veracity of his testimony and, by extension, that of other government officials. More significant is the fact that by his actions Hill implicitly condemned the chief before bringing him to trial. He confirmed for the women, many of these from other areas of Eastern Nigeria, that the Government would easily capitulate to their demands for the removal of unpopular warrant chiefs. It is important to keep in mind that from this time onward the women in other areas were more forward in pressing not only their initial demand that they be exempt from taxation, but also that certain chiefs be dismissed immediately. At Bende on December 2, they formed an opinion of the strength of the Government which was not to be dispelled until after many women had died.

Only after he had surrendered to the women did Hill wire for police reinforcements, and a detachment of twelve men arrived on December 3. The District Officer then decided to try Okugo immediately. While the trial was being conducted inside the court, some three thousand women sat quietly around the Government buildings. This was another example of the firm control which the leaders exercised over the demonstrators. On Wednesday morning, December 3, Okugo was found guilty of two charges. One was spreading news likely to cause alarm, and the other physical assault on the women demonstrators. The unfortunate chief was sentenced to two years' imprisonment. The women of Oloko dispersed, having succeeded in their two objectives, and they played only a very minor role thereafter in the disturbances.

The other alleged culprit from the women's viewpoint was the census taker, Emeruwa. His trial was not the hasty drumhead type as was Okugo's. It began on December 7 and continued throughout the period of the disturbances, concluding on February 27, 1930. Despite the number of witnesses called, the case came down to the conflicting testimony of the woman, Nwanyeruwa, and Emeruwa since there had been no actual witnesses to the affair in Ojim's compound. The court believed Nwanyeruwa and Emeruwa was sentenced to three months in prison.

Even before the trial of Emeruwa began, Captain Hill was attempting to use the responsible women from Bende and Oloko to stop the further spread of disorder. He learned on December 4 that some of the women who had been at Bende earlier had arrived at Umuahia and had caused further disturbances. Hill telegraphed the manager of the United Africa Company at Umuahia to circulate as widely as possible the Government's disclaimer of any plans to tax women. He then called the three leaders of the Oloko-Bende movement and asked them why they were not controlling their followers. The leaders stated that they did not know of any trouble and had not given their permission for further action. They promised to go immediately and stop further violence. On the following day, Hill, accompanied by eighteen police, went to Umuahia. On their way they passed large crowds of women proceeding in all directions. Upon arriving at the town they found only a few women still there.[23]

By December 7, the disturbances in Bende Division were for practical purposes ended. While the rest of Owerri Province was being torn by demonstrations, Bende remained relatively calm. Hill, the police, and some troops continued to make tours in the area through the month of December, more to keep in touch with the situation than to respond to active disturbance. There were only two major breaches of the peace in Bende Division after December 7. On December 12, women destroyed the Ayaba Native Court, and on the 19th and 20th the women gathered again at Umuahia where they forced the warrant chiefs to surrender their caps. A show of force on the part of the Government was all that was necessary to bring these two places once again under control.

Nwanyeruwa, the woman who had first raised the alarm, had become something of a heroine. From all the Ngwa clan towns in Aba and Owerri divisions, money poured into Oloko, given to her by grateful women. Despite her popularity and value as a symbol, she was content to allow leadership in Bende to be exercised by someone else. The money collected was used not for her personally, but to finance trips for delegates to meetings of women throughout the East.[24]

As noted before, the initial demonstrations were tightly controlled and once their objects had been achieved the women returned to their normal habits. The best evidence of the con-servative nature of their thought is their reaction to the news of the violence and looting at Aba. On December 13, they sent the following telegram:

FROM: *Oloko Women*

To: *Aba Women*
       c/o District Officer

Please inform our women friends there stop evils they are doing thats not our objects the tax matter is settled to our satisfaction nothing like houses destroying at Oloko where tax matter first started.[25]

By this time the protest had spread throughout the East almost totally uncontrolled. Women elsewhere struck out blindly against the authorities who had been responsible for old wrongs and who they believed were finally going to destroy them. Failing to have strong leaders, governed by emotion and hatred, and believing that they were safe from harm, the women throughout Owerri and northern Calabar provinces turned to the business of destroying the warrant chiefs and the Native Courts.

CHAPTER VI

The Spread of the Revolt

The disturbances occasioned by the attempted census at Oloko were the focal point for the activities of the women throughout the East. From here the resistance spread, not even to be checked by the capitulation of the women of Bende Division. As early as November 27, a delegation of between fifty and sixty women had left Oloko by train for Port Harcourt to see the resident. In his later testimony, Weir, who met them because the resident was busy, indicated how far the women had already gone with the spreading of the news. They told him that "some women had already gone to Calabar and Onitsha and others were scattered all over the country, complaining of the counting of women and of their goats, sheep and other articles. . . ." [1] The meeting of November 25 in Oloko also brought women delegates from almost every part of the East. Some of these returned immediately to their own villages with the news; others stayed on and took an active part in the demonstrations which resulted in the deposition of Okugo.

There is sufficient evidence to show that these women, far

I

from being satisfied with the favorable solution of the problems at Oloko, were merely encouraged to apply the same pressures on chiefs and government in their areas. At Umuahia on December 6, women from Aba stated that "they didn't want matters to end." They wanted all Native Court members in Owerri Province "to be taken away and to burn all the Native Courts." [2] The Umuahia women reportedly drove these more radical foreign women away by force. It is obvious, nevertheless, that what was merely spoken in Bende Division would serve as a guide for these women once they returned home.

Meanwhile, in Calabar Province a situation was developing remarkably similar to that which had already occurred in Oloko. In Opobo Division another cadet, R. H. Floyer, had taken very seriously the memoranda sent down by higher authority on the subject of reassessment. [3] As early as November 3 he had begun a recount of the Ikpa Clan in the Essene Native Court Area and had encountered no overt opposition. However, by the time he had moved to Ukam on December 1, the news of the Oloko affair had already reached the people. On the following day he addressed the Native Court and explained the reasons for his visit. He then proceeded to Ikot-Obio-Itong to make a trial count. The women of the village followed him about, cursing. Floyer barely escaped being assaulted.

The following day the district officer, A. R. Whitman, arrived in Ukam and held a series of meetings with Floyer and some of the chiefs. Upon his return to Opobo he sent police reinforcements, bringing the total number available in the Ukam area to twelve. All the chiefs of the district were present at a conference at Ukam on December 4. Despite the assurances of the administration that women were not to be taxed, the chiefs refused to take part in the reassessment. They were afraid of the women and obviously did not believe the Government's assurances that their land and palm trees were not going to be confiscated. Later in the afternoon the women rioted, demolished the Essene Native Court, and released a number of men prisoners.

The serious nature of the women's protests was recognized even before December 4, but the senior resident, E. M.

Falk, had to wait for police reinforcements before moving strongly against the demonstrators. On the 5th he arrived at Essene with fifty-six police. By this time the revolt had spread to include all the towns in the vicinity. Thus Falk had to divide his forces to deal with a number of separate disturbances. However, with the arrival on December 8 of an additional thirty police, order of a sort was restored and the damaged buildings could be repaired.[4] It is at this juncture that news of the riots at Aba reached the south and this restarted the revolts in Calabar Province with an intensified violence.

An observer of the disturbances must keep in mind the intertwined nature of the various riots. Just as later the events of Aba were to trigger the most violent protests in Calabar, the reports of the events at Essene were carried north to Aba and Owerrinta. Here the Calabar messengers joined with those who had taken part in the earlier successful movement at Oloko. It would have been surprising, considering the importance of Aba and its location central to the riots in the north and south, if there had not been active protests by the women there. On December 9 there began at Owerrinta the first violence which soon was transferred to Aba. The disturbances at Aba gave the name to the popularized version of all the riots in both provinces.

Aba in 1929 was a moderately large town, remarkably well served by communication links. Four major roads, one each from Owerri, Ikot-Ekpene, Opobo, and Asa led into Aba. In addition it was on the railroad that connected Port Harcourt with the North. Therefore Aba acted as a lodestone for rumors and was easily accessible to people from all over Owerri Province.

The first disturbance occurred in the Owerrinta Native Court Area northwest of the town of Aba on December 9. The assistant district officer was not able to keep the women from releasing prisoners from the jail and doing some damage to property. Jackson, the district officer, went to Owerrinta on the next day but the women would neither disperse nor state their grievances. He was informed that they would tell these to the Government after the meeting of all the Ngwa women scheduled for the next day at the market of the village of Eke-Apara. They had been summoned in Nwanyeruwa's name to choose delegates for a further meeting to be held at Amorji where Nwanyeruwa was to be present. The women at Owerrinta told Jackson that they would call upon him on the 14th after the conclusion of their deliberations.[5]

Jackson returned to Aba on the morning of December 11, and later the resident, F. H. Ingles, arrived. Finding that there were only twenty constables in the town, Ingles telegraphed for reinforcements. Meanwhile, beginning early in the morning, band after band of women streamed through Aba on their way to the meeting at Eke-Apara. The inspector of police, noting the numbers leaving Aba, reported that the women were all leaving the township. The women were noisy, some carried sticks, but there had been no violence. This outward tide of women was reversed shortly after ten o'clock and soon a crowd estimated at more than ten thousand angry women was concentrated near the Government offices in Aba. Reports also came in of the looting of Barclay's Bank, the Post Office, the Survey Office, and the African Merchants Store.[6]

The Commission of Inquiry later asked the obvious question. What had occurred to change the attitude of the women? The district officer and the resident in their evidence stoutly maintained that there had been no change since they believed the women had come into Aba with the intention of causing trouble and looting. This is possible, but in all the women's demonstrations before Aba there had been no looting of private property. Any destruction had been directed toward the warrant chiefs and various buildings which to them represented the detested authority. Many witnesses also swore that earlier in the morning most of the women had been relatively peaceful and were not converging on Aba. The Commission's explanation for the changed atmosphere, which in the light of the evidence seems most reasonable, is that an accident occurred which, though small in itself, changed the behavior of the women in Aba and, for that matter, the entire nature of the demonstrations throughout the East.

This minor event concerned the activities of Dr. Hunter

and one of the nursing sisters at the hospital. When Hunter returned from the hospital after his early morning check he met a crowd of over one hundred women. As he drove past, some of the women struck the car with sticks. After having breakfast, Hunter picked up his nurse about 9:45 and drove once again toward the hospital. The crowd of women, which the doctor presumed was the same he had met before, still blocked the road. The doctor drove into the crowd which parted to let him pass. Once into the crowd Hunter noticed that it was much larger than before and he was trapped in his car. The women beat on the car and threw sticks at it. In trying to get through the crowd Hunter swerved the car and it struck two women. He stopped, tried to get out to help, but was prevented by the crowd. Hunter then turned into the Niger Company compound and joined the agent and his wife in the upper part of the house. The crowd smashed his car and two others in the compound. The doctor attempted to go out and attend the injured women and if necessary take them to the hospital but was prevented from doing this. The arrival of a policeman and some other Europeans allowed the doctor and his companions to escape with only minor injuries.[7]

The injured women were later seen by a number of people. One constable stated that both were very badly hurt and looked as if they might die. Women were shouting, "Doctor has killed women of our party," and later more groups would yell, "We are annoyed." The news of the injuries spread rapidly from one group to another. Shortly after the accident, some women in a fury broke into Barclay's Bank and soon looting was widespread. The bands of women marching out of Aba reversed themselves and poured back into the town.

At the district office, Resident Ingles ordered Assistant District Officer E. V. H. Toovey and his orderly to fire over the heads of one large group of women. Other police came to their aid and the compound was cleared. In a number of other places close to the center of town the police, aided by European volunteers, drove the women back down the main roads. Jackson, with five police, at one point found it necessary to fire over the heads of a group of women. At a little past noon most of the women had been forced out of Aba. Guards were established at the bridge and on all the main roads and barbed-wire cordons set up in key places. The tension of the defenders was eased by midafternoon when reinforcements of thirty police arrived from Port Harcourt. Although numbers of women returned to Aba on the 12th and the authorities read the Riot Act to them, the crisis in Aba had been met successfully. Aba later became something of a model by which to judge riot-control actions of other officers. The accident was not too serious, no one had been killed, and the firm action of fifteen Europeans, ten Africans, and twenty police had dispersed a mob estimated at ten thousand women. Few of the investigators, however, realized how close Aba had been to a massacre. If the women had been better organized or had been more truculent, the forces under Ingles could not have restrained them without using guns.

From Aba new waves of violence first spread through the division and then affected the whole province. On December 12 there was rioting at the Imo River and several factories were looted. Native Courts at Azumini, Obohia, and Asa were destroyed. At Omuma Native Court the offices were broken into and prisoners in jail were released.[8] However, by the evening of the 12th the Government had recovered from its initial paralysis and was concentrating its forces to halt the disturbances in Owerri Province. Lieutenant Governor Cyril Alexander arrived and Aba became the Government's command post. Forty-two extra police marched in, bringing the number of police available for duty to over ninety. The next day the first of the soldiers, two platoons, gave the lieutenant governor a real striking force. This was further augmented by the addition of three companies of the Fourth Battalion between December 18 and 20. On the 13th, Owerri Province was declared a "proclaimed area" under the Peace Preservation Ordinance. Although it was not possible to prevent disturbances from occurring—witness the complete burning of the Omuma Native Court on the 18th —the police and soldiers had the situation in the Aba Division generally under control by the 14th. Cautious, judicious leadership by the officers in charge, combined with the quick concentration of police, held destruction to a minimum, and only one person was seriously hurt. In this connection it is worth noting that army units did not arrive until after the crisis had passed and their later employment was strictly controlled by civilian authority.

The meeting at Owerrinta on December 9, which preceded the worst phase of the disturbances at Aba, served also as the beginning of disorders throughout Owerri Division. Women returning from the meeting demonstrated before the Okpala Native Court and only the presence of the district officer prevented the destruction of the court. The following day, Nguru Court and the Ngor Rest House were destroyed and Ferguson wired to Port Hartcourt for police reinforcements. On the 11th, women in all parts of the district were attacking the chiefs, demanding that they surrender their caps of office. By that evening the district officer had received police reinforcements and also one platoon of troops. Ferguson toured the nearby areas with a portion of the police, meeting with women at Olakwo, Ngor, Nguru, and Okpala. Until the morning of December 14, the women had not attempted a mass demonstration in Owerri town. On that day large numbers of women—estimated at three thousand—attempted to enter the town. They were stopped and turned back at the edge of town by a roadblock manned by twenty police. Twice again on the 15th the women attempted to march into town. Each time they were halted by the police. The next day even greater crowds converged on the town from all directions. At 7:30 in the morning the police, using sticks, drove back approximately four thousand women who attempted to enter the town from the north. Later that morning the police, using the same tactics, turned away two columns of an estimated two thousand women each who approached from the north and east.

Failing to move the police, the women then concentrated upon smaller, less well-protected villages. A detachment of troops under Captain McCullough scattered a mob of women at Okpala on December 20. One woman was injured in the fray. At Oba a platoon of soldiers was forced to form a square with bayonets drawn before it could extricate itself. However, platoons of soldiers from Aba and Oguta enabled the administration to restore order by December 22. Regular patrols of police and troops throughout the division continued until the 27th. The situation was considered calm enough for the soldiers to be withdrawn from Owerri on that day.[9]

Elsewhere in Owerri Province there had been a few outbreaks. In Ahoada Division the Umuaturu Native Court and rest house were burned on the 18th, and on December 21, District Officer Cochrane, backed by soldiers, dispersed a mob of women at Igboda. Earlier than this, on December 12, District Officer Weir in Okigwi Division had confronted large groups of women at Obowa and had been forced to release men from jail in order to secure the safety of a warrant chief and his headmen who were held by the women. The last real disturbance in Okigwi Division occurred on December 17 when two mobs of women were driven out of Okigwi town by police and troops using sticks.[10]

Serious as were these events which flashed through Owerri Province, they proved to be mild when compared to the women's riots occurring simultaneously in Calabar Province. Before attempting to sketch the course of events there, one should point again to the weakness of the police force in the Eastern Region. The disturbances in Owerri Province which climaxed on December 13 had drawn the bulk of the police reserve from Calabar Province. Their place was taken by platoons of soldiers rushed in by the Government to help control the riots. The police, although at first confused by having to face mobs of women, soon responded with basic riot-control methods. The soldiers, however, had not been trained in riot control. Thus when they were in a dangerous situation, pressed by crowds of women, their officers reacted by ordering the troops to fire. Although the disturbances in Calabar were potentially no more dangerous than those in Owerri, the loss of life was much higher. It is as impossible to give an integrated account of the events in Calabar Province as it was in Owerri. Too many simultaneous disturbances were occurring for this. Therefore, the descriptions must be segmented, however interconnected they actually were.

In September 1929, the Resident of Calabar sent out a

circular to all district officers establishing certain guidelines for reassessment of the tax rolls. There was no pressure from the resident to accomplish any reassessment within a certain period. In the Abak District of Calabar Province, an area composed largely of Efik people, tentative moves toward a new assessment were made in the latter part of October.[11] Almost all the chiefs in the district registered their strong disapproval of the proposed recount and on November 6, the district officer, Captain H. P. James, announced the postponement of the reassessment. Despite the inactivity of the government in census taking at Abak, the disturbances generated in Owerri Province reached the district on December 12. Word reached district headquarters that a native court had been burned only twenty-seven miles away. The next day Captain James went to Utu-Etim-Ekpo, Ika, and other nearby Native Courts; he took away all the money and left instructions for disposal of court books in case of trouble. On this tour James did not notice any signs of unrest and on the evening of the 13th he sent a report to Resident Falk stating that he did not expect trouble in the Abak District. On the morning of December 14, he was informed that all Government buildings at Utu-Etim-Ekpo had been burned and the Nigerian Products factory had been looted. James quickly went to Uyo where the resident put at his disposal a platoon of the Nigerian Regiment to reinforce the forty-two police already at Abak.

Returning to Abak, the district officer was told by Warrant Chief Akpan Obo that a crowd of women "like ants on the road" were coming. Chief Akpan had tried to halt them and had barely escaped from their wrath. He reported that the women were wearing leaves on their heads, around their waists, and tied to their legs. According to the chief, this indicated that they were prepared to fight. Many of them were carrying sticks and some were armed with machetes. In reply to the chief's warnings, they told him that the white men would do nothing to them and that the soldiers would not shoot women.

A plan of action was decided upon by the senior police commissioner, E. T. P. Ford. Most of the police were arranged to defend the government offices while some police and the soldiers were kept in reserve. There was to be no firing except on order. About 3:30 in the afternoon a crowd of three hundred to four hundred women approached the station from Utu-Etim-Ekpo. Ford went out to talk to them and soon found himself almost surrounded for the women had spread out fan-wise. To escape he fired into the ground ahead of them and other police moving behind him charged the women and broke up the crowd with the butts of their rifles.

Another group of police was detailed to follow the women out of town and see that they did no damage. The women rallied about four hundred yards past the original skirmish area and charged the police. The police were ordered to fire one volley into the ground in front of the advancing women. This did not stop them, nor did a second volley. Only after the third firing did the women break their charge. The police were then ordered back to Abak and the job of following the women was given a detail of twenty-six soldiers commanded by Lieutenant Browning and accompanied by the district officer, Captain James. The troops also had a Lewis rapid-fire gun with them.

The first Commission of Inquiry stated that a local warrant chief, Akpan Umo, was responsible for stirring up the women in the vicinity of Abak. Earlier he had assured them that the Government planned to tax women and from his compound the women had gone directly to the Native Court and burned it. After their repulse in Abak on the 14th, many women gathered near his compound and he sent messages to nearby villages to invite more to come. Most of the evening of the 14th the women danced, sang, and drummed in the vicinity of Akpan's compound. The Commission alleged that the chief told the women that he would be supplying the soldiers with yams and goats on the next morning. The women, at a discreet distance, should follow his boys who were delivering these items and then charge the soldiers. He assured them that the soldiers would not harm them.

Early the next morning James heard the women even before Chief Akpan arrived. The station where his troops had spent the night was at an intersection of four roads and he did not think it could be defended. Therefore he and his men moved out to meet the women. Many of the women were dressed as the day before in old clothes. Some were stripped to the waist and were wearing leaves and carrying sticks. On seeing the troops blocking the road the women rushed forward. James stated later that he was afraid that his small force would be overwhelmed and that if this happened the whole district would have been up in arms. He ordered the leading section of six men to fire two rounds. One or two women were seen to fall, but the others continued forward. The order was then given to the Lewis gunner to fire seven rounds. The first burst was high, the second on the ground, and the third struck the crowd and halted it. The women then retreated—not in panic, but in good order—and finally dispersed just past the town square. The troops followed them closely and when the women had disappeared Captain James ordered the compound of Chief Akpan Umo to be burned as punishment for his role in the affair.

The razing of the compound had hardly been completed when shouting from the Aba road announced the arrival of more women. A court messenger reported to James that even more were coming from the Ika towns. The troops went out to meet the women on the Aba road and were again charged by the women. Seven more rounds were fired from the Lewis gun before the mob broke. The women coming along the Ika road dispersed after hearing that the soldiers had fired on the two previous groups of women.

The clash at Abak on the 14th and at Utu-Etim-Ekpo on the next day ended for all practical purposes the demonstrations in the Abak District, but with a dreadful loss of life. The final casualty list issued by the second Commission of Inquiry fixed the number killed at Abak at three. The two firings at Utu-Etim-Ekpo killed eighteen and wounded an additional nineteen women.[12] On December 16, reconstruction of the Native Court at Utu-Eim-Ekpo was begun and on the following day Captain James moved to Ika and ordered the rebuilding of the Native Court there. James collected a £200 deposit from the people of both areas against their future good behavior. Police and army units continued with routine patrols until

January 9 when the government withdrew most of the extra police. After the violence of December 15th, the Abak area was quiet.

Meanwhile, the situation in Opobo Division of Calabar Province was building to an even bloodier climax.[13] As previously noted, Cadet Floyer had begun reassessment in early November in accordance with the instructions issued by Resident Falk. This work continued unhampered until he arrived at Ukam Native Court area on December 1. There he was menaced by a large crowd of women and was forced to retire. Two days later the district officer, Whitman, and his assistant held a series of meetings attempting to reassure the people that there were no plans for further taxation. Following such a meeting at Ukam on December 4, a riot began, the Native Court was demolished, and prisoners were released from jail. With his small police detachment Harvey could do nothing to stop the women.

From Ukam the disturbance spread, obviously reinforced by the events in Owerri Province. By December 6 there were twenty-four known towns in Opobo Division in open defiance of the Government. Resident Falk, with fifty-six police, moved to Essene and established his headquarters. The police dispersed two mobs of women on the 6th and another disturbance at Ikot-Obio-Itong on the 8th. With the arrival of thirty more police from Port Harcourt on that day, the crisis, although definitely not over in Opobo Division, seemed to be controlled. Then the news of the rioting and looting at Aba reached the area and precipitated a renewal of the women's protests, this time concentrated on Opobo town. The women there had been quiet while their counterparts elsewhere in the division had been causing trouble. District Officer Whitman met with a small delegation of leading women traders of Opobo town on Saturday, the 14th, and arranged to hold a general meeting for all the women on the 16th.

Whitman was in Essene on Sunday, the 17th, presumably to confer with Resident Falk on the conditions of the area. A messenger from Chief Mark Pepple Jaja reached him that evening with the news that the Opobo women had wrecked the dispensary and the Native Court, had looted the postal agency, and had assaulted him and some of the other chiefs. Returning to Opobo, Whitman made the best disposition he could of the thirty-two police at his disposal. He stationed most of the police in strategic locations where they could guard the public buildings. Cadet Floyer reported to him that at seven o'clock in the morning on the 16th he and seven police had just escaped from being completely surrounded by a large group of women. Whitman was later reinforced by Lieutenant J. N. Hill and thirty men of the Nigerian Regiment. Thus strengthened, Whitman decided that he could protect Government Hill and still hold the meeting he had promised the women.

The women had used a place called Doctor's Farm near Opobo Government Station for their staging ground after the attacks of the 15th. From there and from the river large numbers of women pressed forward toward the district offices. Hill marched his troops around the station to let the women know that soldiers were present. From time to time he talked to the crowd at various points. By 8:30, some women had forced their way into the district offices. Others, armed with sticks and machetes, danced outside. The police drove the women from the offices and cleared the area immediately to the front. Under these conditions, with Whitman confronting between one thousand and fifteen hundred women, the meeting began.

Whitman attempted to address the crowd to tell them that the Government had no intention of taxing the women. The noise was so great that he could not be heard except by the women directly in front of him. Some of the leaders complained to him of certain abuses which they wanted corrected and demanded that he put their requests and his assurances down in writing. Not satisfied with this, they then told him that they wanted typewritten copies of his statements. Whitman compiled these and after a time six typed copies of the agreement were given to the leaders. This agreement is important because it is one of the few pieces of written evidence illustrating the grievances of the women against the Government. The document stated:

1. The Government will not tax women.

2. No personal property, such as boxes, is to be counted.

3. Any one woman who is a known prostitute is [not?] to be arrested.

4. Women are not to be charged rent for the use of the common market shed.

5. They ask that licenses for holding plays should not be paid for. I promised to bring this complaint to the notice of the Government.

6. They do not want Chief Mark Pepple to be Head Chief of Opobo Town. I will so inform Government.

7. The women do not want any man to pay tax. I promised to inform Government.

8. They are speaking for Obopo, Bonny and Andoni women.[14]

It was approximately 10:30 before Whitman had signed and given out the typescript to the women. It is doubtful whether women more than a few yards away knew what was going on. As time passed, the yelling increased. One is struck by the lack of order and discipline among the women in Calabar Province as compared with the rigid control exercised by the leaders at Oloko where the disturbances began. To Whitman and Hill it became apparent that the women with whom they had been dealing could not, even had they wanted to, control their followers. Suddenly the mob of women surged forward, breaking through the light protective fence on the left and right. Hill signaled Whitman that he was taking over command and shouted to the women to halt. When they refused and were within a few feet of him, Hill fired at the leading woman and ordered the troops to fire. This halted the central element but a group armed with machetes broke away and charged the post office. A second volley was ordered and after this the crowd broke and ran.

Despite the contention of the second Commission of Inquiry that the firing was not under control, the troops behaved in a most disciplined fashion. There were thirty men and sixty-one rounds were fired. The extra shot had been fired by Hill to open the affair. The results were terrible for this had been point-blank firing. Twenty-six women were killed immediately and thirty-one were wounded. Three of the wounded later died in the hospital and the Commission discovered that three more had died in the villages.[15] To the women of Opobo District this was ample proof that being women was no protection against the Government. They had discovered that soldiers would fire on women and that despite the disparity in numbers, a group of soldiers could disperse a mob one hundred times its size. After the killings at Opobo town on December 16, soldiers and police in the district were engaged only in routine patrols.

There were other centers of disturbance in Calabar Province but none reached dangerous proportions. One reason for this was that in districts such as Itu and Arochukwu the women's reaction was triggered by events at Aba and later Opobo. The strength of their protests was measured by the failure of the women at those places. Also by mid-December, the Government was able to free large numbers of police and soldiers in the pacified areas and virtually flood potential trouble zones with them. For example, in Itu the most dangerous situation developed on December 16 at Okopedi where women started to break into a factory. The Riot Act was read to the women by the commanding officer of the troops and the women dispersed. Similarly at Ntan the next day the women showed no desire for a confrontation when seven police drove off a crowd estimated at over two thousand. In Arochukwu District, the center of the once-feared Aro people, the district officer, Cheesman, maintained order during the crucial period with a special police force made up of fifty-six roadmen. There were many meetings of women in Arochukwu but little destruction. Cheesman was allowed to talk to the women at their meetings and except at Umon Native Court they listened and believed his promises.[16]

By December 20, Calabar Province was under control once again. The activities of the authorities in these areas after this date will be detailed later. It seems proper, after relating the outlines of the disturbances, to return to the questions posed at the beginning of Chapter V—namely, why did the women riot? To reinforce the generalizations made previously, one should refer to the participants and observers and allow them to describe their actions and the reasons for them. Aside from the obvious protest against taxation, the main goal of the women in both Owerri and Calabar provinces was the destruction of the warrant-chief system. Many chiefs seemed surprised at the women's actions—witness the statement of Chief Mark Pepple Jaja of Opobo, that "women never banded together before in that way. If they had grievances they came to the head of their house with the complaint." [17] The chief failed to understand that the women no longer had faith in their political leaders. To go through the motions of complaining in the traditional way would accomplish nothing. The women from the outset were out to destroy the synthetic political system which denied them justice. The cynicism of the women regarding this was pointed out by a woman from Oloko who said, "Chiefs are all alike. When one says a thing, the others all say the same. That is why we made demonstration." [18] As has already been noted, the easy capitulation of the district officer at Bende gave women in both provinces the hope that by acting together they could rid themselves of the chiefs.

One question that has not been answered is the role of the men in the disturbances. The residents of both Calabar and Owerri provinces were convinced that the men were behind the riots, using the women as cats'-paws.[19] Resident Ingles believed that the men had perfected an efficient and thorough organization and were waiting only for the opportunity to put their plans into effect. This opinion was shared by the majority of the district officers. But if this were the case, why did the men not rush to the aid of the women when they had gained a temporary advantage at Oloko, Aba, Abak, and Opobo? There emerged at the second Commission of Inquiry contradictory testimony that men in fairly large numbers had been present at only one place—Opobo.[20] Even there Captain Hill's recollections were countered by other witnesses who stated that they did not see any significant number of men. Many of the women who took part in the demonstrations denied that there was a "master mind" behind the affairs and that men had played an important role in planning. One of the best statements to this effect was given by Akulechula, a woman of Obowo in Okigwi District, who said:

> It has been suggested here that men encouraged women to move about. I deny that statement. It is not true. We were not encouraged by men. . . . It is against native custom for women to leave their houses without permission of their husbands but in this case men had been made to pay tax and the rumor that women were going to be taxed was spread around. Women became infuriated because they had already felt the burden of the tax on men. . . . We acted according to our own consciences. . . . There is no law made by men that women should not move about. The matter did not concern men.[21]

The best answer respecting the men's role seems to be that it was a passive, hopeful one. There can be no doubt that many were shocked by the activities of their women. But the suddenness of the women's victory at Bende counterbalanced this reaction and the men elsewhere adopted a passive attitude since the women would have more of a chance of overawing the Government without the men. There was a widespread feeling that the Government would not harm women. The men knew that the police and soldiers had no such compunction where they were concerned. If the women won as they had at Bende, then the men would win also.

Some comment should be made about the dress and behavior of the women. Reference has already been made to the "Ogbo" and related women's societies as one of the main channels through which the revolt spread. The women also used other traditional signs in their activities. Many of them dressed in old clothes and smeared their faces and bodies with clay. According to Chief Mark Pepple Jaja, this was borrowed from the men. He said, "When men went to war in old times they used to spread clay or such like on their faces. I never saw women doing it before." [22] Another symbol which the women used, particularly in Calabar, was the wearing of leaves on their heads and bodies. Chief Jaja also stated that "wearing or passing palm frond is the sign that the people are out to make

K

trouble." [23] Thus symbolically the women were telling every-one who could read their signs that they were at war with the Government.

Why did the women believe they could succeed? It is im-portant to keep in mind that they had accomplished their goals in Bende Division. In the early stages of the revolt the Gov-ernment and the detested warrant chiefs seemed to be too weak to resist them. There was also a strange mixture of fatalism and optimism in the crowds of women. At Owerrinta on December 7, a native minister, Pastor Inyama, remembered women singing mournful songs similar to those sung when a calamity had over-taken the country. He recalled one of these, "We are dying. Our hearts are not good, for Death is standing before us." [24] At Umuaturu in Ahoada Division some of the women chanted as they destroyed the Native Court, "It is not by our own power that we are doing this. God has sent us to do this thing." [25]

Their optimism was based upon the past actions of men toward women as well as a metaphysical certainty that God would protect them. Most of them sincerely believed that "women cannot be killed." In some cases this was because they felt themselves the "spirit of womanhood (*Oha Ndi Nyiom*)" [26] and were therefore inviolable. In Calabar Province particularly they called themselves vultures, and chanted about these scav-engers: "Vultures are coming to the feast." One woman of Utu-Etim-Ekpo explained this allusion and also registered her shock that the soldiers would harm women. She said, "I was surprised to see the soldiers fire as we were women. We call ourselves vultures as we did not think soldiers would fire on us. Vultures go to the market to eat food there and nobody molests them; nobody will kill a vulture even in the market, even if it kills fowls." [27]

These myths of invincibility were shattered by the deaths at Abak and Opobo. The optimism was destroyed. After those events no woman in a mob could comfort herself with the idea that she was protected from injury or death. Such knowledge, combined with the growing number of police and soldiers, dic-tated a halt to the demonstrations. In this connection the men in the disaffected areas probably played a decisive role. One administrative officer confirmed this when he noted:

> The men were more affected than the women by the measures taken to restore order in this Division and there is little doubt that the women, when they realized that their demands for abolition of tax would not be granted would have made determined attempts at further mass demonstrations had they not been restrained by their menfolk.[28]

With the ending of the women's demonstrations the Government was once again in firm control of the two provinces, but the faith in the soundness of the warrant-chief system which had motivated the higher echelons to proceed with taxation had been rudely shaken. The violence and bloodshed underscored the warnings given by many junior civil servants in the years preceding the riots. Even while pacification was continuing in the latter days of December 1929, the Government for the first time realized just how bad conditions were in the Eastern areas. It finally began to act on the statement made by S. M. Grier in 1922 that the most important factor in the complex eastern situation was that the Government admit its past mistakes and attempt to correct them.

CHAPTER   VII

The Government's Reaction

The first task confronting Sir Graeme Thomson's shaken administration in the latter part of December 1929 was to make certain that the women, now reasonably quiet, did not create new disturbances. Owerri and Calabar provinces had both been declared "disaffected areas" under the Peace Preservation Ordinance which gave powers to the civil and police authorities much greater than usual.[1] At the discretion of the administration a village could be required to pay a deposit of money as a bond for its future good behavior, or the Government could demand supplies for the police or soldiers in lieu of a deposit. The areas affected by the women's riots were also placed under the Collective Punishment Ordinance.[2] This gave the authorities the right to assess fines for suspected wrongdoing or past actions on a collective rather than individual basis. Fines could be imposed on villages or a whole district up to the amount of damage caused by the people in the area. The Government could also confiscate property to enforce its demands, and the district officer could order a compound or a series of compounds burned either as punishment or as an object lesson to others. The regular police in the two provinces had been augmented by the bulk of the special police force recruited for such an outbreak in 1928. In addition, most of the troops of the Fourth Battalion of the West Africa Frontier Force, normally stationed in Western Nigeria, had joined their eastern counterpart, the Third Battalion.[3] Thus the Government had enough force to implement its retaliatory actions.

District officers, accompanied by troops and police, were concerned primarily with crushing every sign of further resistance and overawing traditional leaders with a display of strength. The patrols that continued at full strength through January 10 served this purpose well although there was no attempt made to rationalize punishment from one area to another to correlate with damage done. The fines assessed were much higher in Owerri Province than elsewhere, with the officials in Aba Division demanding the highest payments. At Owerrinta Native Court Area of Aba Division, a fine of ten shillings per adult male or £2,355 was levied. At Ngor and Nguru the fines were respectively three shillings and five shillings, three pence per adult male. In the Obohia area where the Native Court was burned, the people were assessed £2,847, the equivalent of one pound for every adult male. This amounted to three times the tax rate and five times as much as that recommended for the people of Umuaturu Native Court who had caused about the same amount of damage.[4] A £2,000 fine was assessed at Azumini town which was six times the annual tax rate. Furthermore, payment of the full sum was demanded within forty-eight hours. The district officer justified this because he felt that the Azumini people had been primarily responsible for spreading the disorders to Abak and Opobo.[5] Although these are examples of the extremes in application of the Collective Punishment Ordinance, fines were assessed all over Owerri and Calabar provinces. The fines that were levied in January were all collected by the end of June. By then the Governor had approved a 40 per cent remission of the amounts originally assessed.

Compounds were demolished or burned as another example of the power of the Government. Although this practice was not widespread, it was used against the villages of Ibuaku in

Calabar Province and Alayi, Umuakpara, and Obuzza in Owerri Province.[6] There were also cases of willful mishandling of demands for provisioning of troops. At Azumini a company of troops was supported by the townspeople for eight days. No receipts were given and no records kept of the supplies consumed so that this could be deducted later from the fine.[7]

Apart from the punitive expeditions, the Government was faced with a reoccurrence of the disturbances in many areas in early 1930. In Afikpo Division of Ogoja Province and at Umuchieze in Onitsha Province only the prompt action of administrative officers averted real problems.[8] At Aloyi in Bende Division in January and at Isoba in Ahoada Division in May, women attempted to seize the caps of unpopular warrant chiefs. As late as October 1930, there was a serious situation at Mbidi near Oguta. This concerned dissatisfaction over Government regulations for determining the purity of palm oil. Before this reaction was crushed, one man was killed and several were wounded by the police.[9] Although these isolated cases of anti-Government activity continued throughout the year, the disaffected areas were calm enough for the Peace Preservation Ordinance to be withdrawn in late February.

The second problem facing Governor Thomson was to find out what had caused the women to revolt. Two imperatives demanded that this be done immediately. One was to provide the Colonial Office and Parliament with appropriate answers to their questions.[10] The other was the necessity to find out the weaknesses of the Eastern system so that changes could be instituted to remove the danger of the riots' reoccurring. On January 2, 1930, therefore, Governor Thomson appointed a Commission of Inquiry, naming two men to investigate the disturbances at Opobo, Abak, and Utu-Etim-Ekpo which had been responsible for the greatest loss of life.[11] The two members of the commission were Major William Gray, Administrator of the Colony, and Henry Blackall, a legal expert. They opened hearings at Opobo an January 6 and moved to Abak four days later. The Commission held sittings at Abak and Utu-Etim-Ekpo and closed their investigations on January 17. In this brief time it heard the testimony of thirty-six witnesses. Its short report of fourteen pages with fifty-two pages of attached "minutes of evidence" was filed with the Government on January 27. Very few of the witnesses called represented native opinion and still fewer represented persons who had played an active part in the riots.

Nevertheless, considering how important was the time factor, the report of this first Commission was very informative. The much more exhaustive investigations of the second Commission added little to the facts of the Calabar disturbances as presented by Gray and Blackall. The significant differences concerned assessment of the guilt of the government officers involved in the shootings. The first Commission found that all administrative officers, police, and soldiers had acted responsibly and, however unfortunate the results, there could be no question of castigating the officers for their actions.

Even before the report of the first Commission was made public, it was obvious that a far more thorough investigation of the events in the disaffected areas would be necessary. In response to this need, Governor Thomson on February 7 appointed a second, six-man Commission of Inquiry, headed by Donald Kingdon, the Chief Justice. Other members were Sir Kitayi Ajasa; barrister; William Hunt, Resident; Graham Paul, Advocate, Eric Olowolu Moore, barrister; and Ronald Osborne, Agent General, John Holt and Company. The members of this Commission were not only extremely well qualified, the Europeans all having had years of experience in Southern Nigeria, but they were unlikely to reflect Government opinion automatically. The only official spokesman for the Government, Hunt, was more than counterbalanced by the presence of two Africans on the Commission.[12]

The Commission was charged to investigate two different although correlated problems. The first was to inquire into the causes of the disturbances in both Calabar and Owerri Provinces and the measures taken to restore order there, and to make any recommendations concerning these affairs as they saw fit. The second charge was to inquire into the responsibility of any person or persons who failed to anticipate the disturbances and to take adequate precautions to safeguard life and property.

The Commission formally opened at Aba on March 10. Twelve public sittings were held at Aba, nine at Umudiko, and four at Owerri in Owerri Province. In Calabar Province seven days were spent at Opobo and five at Ekot-Ekpene. An additional sitting was held at Lagos. The Commission heard a total of 485 witnesses. The people in Owerri Province proved eager to give evidence. At the three towns in Owerri Province where the Commission convened, the halls were filled to capacity and frequently many thousands, mostly women, congregated outside. In Calabar Province there were smaller crowds and fewer witnesses. The Commission noted that the people seemed more cowed in Calabar than in Owerri. The long, extremely thorough report, complete with such items as a forty-seven page memorandum by the secretary of the Southern Provinces, C. T. Lawrence, was presented to the Government on July 21, 1930. All the members of the commission signed the document, but two members, Graham Paul and Ronald Osborne, filed separate reservations on specific points.[13]

In brief the Commission found that the riots had been occasioned by the introduction of taxation and the precipitate actions of some administrative officials. In Bende Division the concealment from the people of the reasons for the assessment in 1926 and 1927 laid the foundation for the women's suspicions in 1929. The Commission held Resident Ingles responsible for this. In the same division the indiscriminate count of women, children, and livestock in late 1929 was the immediate cause of the disturbances. The acting district officer, Cook, was blamed for this development. The surrender by District Officer Hill of Okugo's cap to the women at Bende was considered a terrible mistake. Taken in conjunction with the hasty trial of the chief and the assessor Emeruwa, it gave the impression of Government weakness. At Aba they condemned the district officer for not calling for reinforcements sooner and gave as their opinion that the accidental death of some women transformed basically peaceful groups of women into a hostile, looting mob.

Their findings in Calabar Province were of the same order. The hasty reassessment throughout the region was blamed upon the resident, Falk. On a smaller though more important scale the recounts in the Essene and Ukam areas were blamed upon the district officer, Whitman, and on Cadet Floyer. The first Commission had found the shooting unfortunate but necessary. The second, however, in a point-by-point recitation, condemned the actions that had led to the killing of the women. They found that defense measures were inadequate at the Imo River and they were extremely critical of the disposition of police and soldiers at Opobo. They singled out individual officers for blame in each of the occurrences.

The main report was not critical of the central government. Only a few of their recommendations touched upon the responsibility of the governor and his immediate staff in the Eastern areas. For instance, they noted that the special force of police recruited as insurance against disturbances arising from taxation had been reduced "in the disaffected areas below the margin of safety." The Commission held the lieutenant governor responsible for this. They also noted, almost in passing, that the work load imposed upon administrative officers was too heavy and recommended that they be relieved of some of the "busy work" so that they would have more time to devote to the more important aspects of their jobs. It was also remarked that the Government should take appropriate steps to insure continuity of service in the Eastern districts.

The central government, however, did not escape unscathed. Graham Paul, in his tightly reasoned reservation, went below the surface events and laid the blame for the riots directly upon the shortsighted policies of Governor Thomson and his advisers. He disagreed with his colleagues in faulting individual officers for their "excess zeal," quoting Resident Falk who had reported the reluctance of his officers to begin work connected with taxation. On this point Paul wrote, "There seems to me, however, the tendency to cover up what I consider to be the real fundamental mistake by attaching blame to officers for the very efficiency and thoroughness with which they endeavoured to carry out the mistaken policy." [14]

To Paul the "fundamental mistake" was taxation itself. He noted, "I think that in fact the taxation was introduced long before preliminary work had been completed. It is not yet completed." [15] The so-called "intelligence side" of assessment had been almost completely ignored. The central government had paid little attention to the problem of discovering the "natural rulers" of the people upon whose authority the entire system of indirect rule and taxation ultimately depended. Instead, it had adopted without question certain assumptions inherited from Lord Lugard, the most damaging being the dictum about the need for taxation as a preliminary for education in the art of self-government. On this point Paul wrote, "On the contrary it seems to me that very considerable progress in the most essential part of this political "education" *could* and *should* have been made before the introduction of direct taxation." [16]

Stress has been placed upon Paul's dissent for two reasons. He was the only man on the Commission who saw clearly that however guilty individual officers might have been in precipitating the disturbances, their actions were only contributory. The main fault lay in the system imposed by the central Government. In this analysis he was echoing reservations to government policy expressed hesitatingly by a number of junior administrative officers in 1927. The second reason for noting Paul's criticisms is that his ideas were accepted, perhaps unknowingly, by the Secretary of State for the Colonies, Lord Passfield, and by Governor Thomson's successor, Sir Donald Cameron.

Recommendations made by the Commission for future action by the Government were generally pragmatic and conservative. They did not attempt to outline what future policy should be, but contented themselves with answers to specific problems. [17] Among the most important suggestions were the release of Okugo and Emeruwa, de-emphasis of the revenue aspect of taxation, ending the practice of assessing the number of men by ratio to houses, doors, etc., and reevaluation of the tax in light of the fall in the price of palm produce. The Commission recognized that the native-court system was faulty and suggested that a special commission be appointed to investigate its operations. The Commission further suggested gradually eliminating the warrant chiefs whose appointment did not reflect their role in traditional society. It had no formula for the selection of new chiefs except to note that perhaps they could be selected by a more democratic process on the village levels. The Commission warned the Government against any hasty action in replacing warrant chiefs who had been created by government fiat. There should be no wholesale suspension or dismissal of warrant chiefs, particularly when the Eastern areas were still not completely pacified.

Actions taken by the Government by 1930 to remedy the most glaring defects of the Eastern political system will be detailed later. It is necessary first to trace the further history of the Commission's report and see what effect, if any, it had on Colonial policy. On January 31, 1931, a long debate on the report was held in the Legislative Council. An African member of the Council moved that the Government express regrets for the loss of life in the disturbances and that the officers censured by the Commission be punished. The senior administrative officers on the Council defended the actions of the men singled out by the report. They stressed the guilt of the women in precipitating the confrontations and the great strain under which the administrative staff in the East had to work. The Government made it clear that it would accept the first part of the motion but not the second. On this basis the first part was carried while the second lost by a vote of thirty-five to two. Five Africans voted with the Government on this division.[18]

The punitive aspects of the report were laid to rest finally in February 1931 by the comments of the Secretary of State for Colonies.[19] Lord Passfield stated that he would not welcome any further investigations into the activities of individual officers involved in the disturbances. The situations that confronted these men had been so unusual that they could have had no previous experience to rely upon. He could not judge, far removed as he was, under what circumstances firing into the crowds had been necessary.

After dismissing this phase of the report, Passfield then delivered his own summation of the causes for the disturbances.

He did not completely ignore the bulky record of the second Commission but his critique was of the same nature as Graham Paul's dissent. He stated, "It appears to me that it was probably injudicious and premature to introduce into these Provinces a system of direct taxation without first completing a more intensive survey of their social organization." [20]

Passfield noted that both Grier and Tomlinson had indicated the need for such exhaustive studies and their advice had been ignored, he commented, "I cannot refrain from a feeling that inadequate attention was paid to the views of the officers in immediate contact with the districts concerned, when the introduction of the measure of direct taxation was under consideration." [21]

His indictment of the actions of the central government continued by pointing out that the Eastern areas had been neglected. The Government had seemingly concluded that the problem of languages in the East was "insuperable" and that of continuity of administration was "insoluable." Therefore the Government devoted more of its time and energies to the less complex areas of the North and West. In the best formal, polite language, Passfield placed the direct responsibility for the riots upon Governor Thomson and his immediate staff. Passfield noted that the Secretary of State at the time of the imposition of taxes had given permission to the Governor to proceed. This had been based, however, on the presumption that the views of the Governor and his advisers were sound. [22]

Governor Thomson's administration had been forced by the riots to confront the inadequacies of its policies in the East and had begun in early 1930 a serious restudy of native administration. There were many factors which dictated to the Government a slow and cautious attitude. First the policing action in the wake of disturbances had to be completed before any serious changes could be made. Also the taxes for the year 1930 had to be collected. The second Commission of Inquiry did not complete its report until midyear. Until this had been done, the Government could not be sure of the causes of the riots, let alone begin to alter the system to prevent their recurrence. Further, there was the problem of Governor Thomson himself. He was nearing the end of his period in office and, as has been indicated, the Colonial Office was none too pleased with the results of his policy. It is doubtful whether it would have approved any major revision of the political system of the Eastern Region suggested by Governor Thomson. In the fall of 1930 the Governor returned to London and his place in Nigeria was filled temporarily by the lieutenant governor for the Southern Provinces, Captain W. Buchanan-Smith. Buchanan-Smith had only been appointed to the post in August when C. W. Alexander, the previous officeholder, was appointed as the lieutenant governor of the Northern Provinces.[23] Thus by the fall of 1930 the two men most responsible for government policy in the East were no longer in positions of command in Southern Nigeria. Any sweeping revision of the system would have to await the arrival of the new Governor.

This does not mean the Government did not undertake any useful projects in 1930. The broad guidelines of some of the necessary changes had been laid out by the second Commission of Inquiry. C. T. Lawrence, the secretary of the Southern Provinces, had indicated in his memorandum of January 16 how sweeping the changes would have to be. He had written of the Native Courts, "The only sure remedy to cure the evil [abuses in the system] completely would be the entire removal of these opportunities [for graft] and probably the abolition of the Native Courts and a reversion to some crude form of local village council, would be the only way to attain this end." [24]

Lawrence believed that such a complete reversal of policy would have been too drastic to apply immediately, even had conditions been normal. With the East in a disturbed state, such a remedy was clearly impossible. He believed it best to effect a compromise with the existing system by adjusting native court areas to make them, wherever possible, coterminous with clan boundaries. This was to be accompanied by a thorough search by administrative officers of their areas to determine the character of the traditional political and legal system. Whenever a traditional leader or leaders were found, the Government should officially recognize their right to rule. Warrant chiefs who did not have the respect of their people should not be dismissed immediately. To do this would leave the impression that the Government was surrendering to the threat of violence. Rather, such warrant chiefs should be removed gradually from office.[25]

Lawrence's memo became the guide for the actions of the Government, whether consciously or not on their part, in the two years following the disturbances. Aside from pacification measures, primacy was given to collecting information. The administrative staff was ordered to make detailed studies of the people in their areas and to recommend changes in the political and judicial establishment. This was, in reality, a continuation of the investigations that had preceded taxation with the important difference that now the Government was more concerned with the people than with the imposition of a system of taxation. Despite obvious reluctance on the part of some Colonial Office officials, Dr. C. K. Meek, the Anthropological Officer for the Northern Provinces, was sent to the Eastern area to advise the administration and also to carry out his own independent research.[26] His greatest service was as an adviser. Most of the reports made by district officers were sent to Meek for his comments before the Government would act on the recommendations. Meek did two thorough investigations himself, one at Nsukka and the other of Owerri Division.[27] The pressure of his other duties and the volume of anthropological investigation to be completed tended to minimize the effect that his own reports had on Government reforms.

The bulk of the 144 "intelligence reports" submitted by the end of 1933 were done by administrative officers.[28] These officers had not been trained in anthropology and most did not know the languages sufficiently well to do thoroughgoing studies. Even had the district officers possessed all the necessary qualifications, they would not have had the time to produce such reports. Conditions in the East were such that the officers had to compile and evaluate their data quickly. The studies had limited and practical goals since the Government was concerned primarily with the mainsprings of traditional political and judicial organizing among the Ibo and Ibibio people.

District officers soon discovered and passed on to higher authority the discrepancy between the political functions of native leaders, as envisioned by the Government, and their judicial powers. In traditional society there had not been a genuine separation of these, and if Britain had decided to scrap all of its previous work perhaps there need not have been a distinction. However, the Governor and his advisers wanted to keep intact as much of the preriot court system as possible. Clearly they could not do this and still give political power to traditional rulers who were only clan and sometimes even village leaders. In order to mold local government more in conformity with the native political system, many "native authorities" would have to be created. The pre-1930 forced wedding between the Native Court and the political leaders could be maintained only by decentralizing the courts and this the Government did not wish to do. The hope was that wherever possible the Native Court could be maintained and new courts would be added only when it was necessary to rectify previous errors of ignoring clans. The most serious problem was realigning native-court boundaries so that each court would, as far as possible, represent a clan. The major reform in the court system was to be in the composition of the court. The Government hoped, by cutting the power of the court clerks and supplying warrants only for natural leaders, that most of the abuses complained of by the people would soon disappear. As reform proceeded it became clear that reorganization of the Native Courts would be more complex than this. Then, too, the new Governor, Sir Donald Cameron, after his evaluation of Native Courts throughout Nigeria, asked for a more flexible representative system. The policy of dealing with the "native authorities" and the courts as separate although closely connected entities, however, had been established in practice before the arrival of the new Governor.

The selection of Cameron to be Governor of Nigeria at this crucial period was one of the most astute decisions made by any Colonial Secretary. Few men in the Colonial service had had more direct experience in Nigeria. In January 1908, he was appointed assistant secretary of Southern Nigeria and until September 1924, when he relinquished the position of chief secretary to become Governor of Tanganyika, he had been intimately connected with the upper echelons of Nigerian government. He was a protégé and in a sense a disciple of Lugard in that he believed the best system of local government for Africans to be that with which they were most familiar. Unlike many of his contemporaries, Cameron did not view such government as primitive or static. If properly handled, "native administration," a term he preferred to "indirect rule," would become the means of reconciling traditional methods with Western concepts.[29] This meant that British administration must make every effort to understand the divergent societies over which they held control and to encourage the natural leaders of the people in the exercise of their authority. Cameron's record in governing Tangyanyika attested to the soundness of this pragmatic philosophy.

It is obvious that Lord Passfield, impressed by Cameron's success in Tanganyika, concluded that conditions in Nigeria could be improved only by a comparable approach. Although Cameron was notified of his appointment in December 1930, he did not actually arrive in Nigeria to take up his post until early 1931. He then devoted much of his time in the first months to reeducating himself on the Nigerian situation. Every assessment report on the East that had been submitted for the period 1926 through 1928 shows in his pungent marginal comments the signs of his careful reading. From the later reforms that he instituted we know that he was extremely unhappy about the administration in every region of Nigeria and not just the Eastern territories. The East, however, was the most crucial area. Cameron was very careful in his few published works later not to assign blame to any individual for the sad state of Nigeria.[30] Some of his statements, however, show clearly his dissatisfaction and also his pragmatic approach. He wrote:

> In Southern Nigeria in the old days when the primary consideration was to open up the country, that trade and revenue might follow and allow the new dependency to be self supporting, the Calabar Government did not think of finding the real leaders of the people—perhaps they had no time for that kind of thing—and used as

L

their medium for intercourse with the people the loudest-mouthed ruffian that presented himself to their notice.[31]

In contrast to this type of local authority, Cameron recommended to the government: "Build from the bottom; do not attempt as I found in Nigeria when I returned there in 1931 to make as it were, a crown or a king at the top and then try to find something underneath on which it might—perhaps—appropriately be placed." [32] The debased system of native administration in Nigeria was further castigated in his warning, "Shun as you would evil the make-believe 'Indirect Administration' based on nothing that is really true. It is a monster and a very dangerous one at that." [33]

Thus after 1931 Nigeria was led by a man with most definite opinions on native administration who placed primary emphasis on the knowledge of and respect for indigenous institutions. He pushed the residents and district officers ahead in the task, already begun, of gathering intelligence reports and was not afraid, out of a preconceived idea that large administrative units were necessarily superior, of recognizing small units as Native Authorities.

The intelligence reports from almost all parts of Owerri Province in 1932 showed that there were no real functioning Native Authorities anywhere. Aba Division, for example, was divided into seven native-court areas, none of which were natural units. The same conditions obtained for Bende, Owerri, and Ahoada Divisions. Yet the village organization by then was fairly well known throughout the province.[34] District officers encouraged the functioning of village councils which usually were the highest unit of native administration. Members of these councils met to handle such local affairs as tax assessments, maintenance of roads, and plans for future village development. Matters affecting the whole division were discussed by meetings of representatives of these village councils in each native-court area. From most of these councils the warrant chiefs who had been so important in local government prior to 1930 were generally excluded unless they also had the sanction of the people.[35]

In Calabar Province much the same situation prevailed in

1931 as in Owerri. The resident noted that there was no native administration, as he understood that term, functioning in the entire province. He declared in explanation of this statement:

> Throughout the Tribes which inhabit the Province the unit is the village, or among the Efiks and Opobos, the "House." Cohesion between groups or villages due to common ancestry or worship, exists and allows the formation of Village Groups and Clans; but nowhere in the Province is there to be found a Group, Clan, or Tribal Head whose authority is recognized by the people or one whose power could be used as a focus for local administration.[36]

In Calabar the district officers were beginning, however, to use village and clan representatives for closer communication with the people. There was considerable difficulty in establishing Native Administrations among the Efik in Calabar largely due to jealousies between the families of the Etuboms, or heads of houses.[37]

The Government was aided in its attempt to establish *de facto* councils based on kindred, villages, and clans in this transition period because during the long period of the warrant chiefs they had continued to exist. Now that the decision to phase out the previous system had been made, the Government was simply prepared to recognize these agencies as the real local government of the East. The easy transition to the new decentralized "native authority" is in itself an indictment of the failure of the British-imposed warrant-chief system.

The reorganization of the Native Authorities in the East by the end of 1934 presented a totally different governing structure from that of two years before. Throughout Owerri Province, wherever possible, administrative and court divisions were based on clan divisions and below this group, on the lowest level, the village. How complex this type of organization could appear is easily seen when one remembers that in Aba Division alone there were five distinct clans and dozens of villages. Before the reorganization of the province was completed there would be 245 Native Authorities and subauthorities.[38] The same complexity was noticeable in Calabar Province. By the end of 1934 there were forty-six clans in Calabar Province, at least thirteen of which had not yet been recognized by the Government.[39] Some idea of how inflated and seemingly unwieldy the Native Authorities had become is shown by the organization of the Calabar Council which represented approximately 40,000 people. It consisted of: [40]

16	Etuboms (heads of Houses)	Efik
119	Advisers	
9	Ntoes (Headmen)	Kwa
12	Representatives	
5	Muris (Headmen)	Efut
6	Representatives	
167		

To the observer used to small councils presided over by a permanent chief, the new units of government in the East appeared to be chaotic. This, however, was not the case. The Ibo and the majority of Ibibio people were accustomed to such large representative bodies. The size of the councils guaranteed that no one man, such as the old native-court clerk, could dominate and force his opinions on the people. Decisions taken by councils on any level were acceptable to the governed since they could see that these had been arrived at by their own leaders and not by the fiat of a few favored by the British administrator.

A task correlative with reconstruction of native administration was the reorganization of the court system. Prior to the women's disturbances, Owerri and Calabar provinces had been divided into a few native-court areas. Each of these courts normally exercised jurisdiction over different clans and in some cases different tribal groups. In many of the courts the clerk exercised powers far beyond the intention of the British administrators, and the warrant chiefs certainly did not have the confidence of the people. In most districts the numbers of warrant chiefs assigned to a court area were too many to work efficiently together if all were to sit at one time. Therefore the practice had developed of selecting only four warrant chiefs to handle all cases in a Native Court for a month.[41] Even before the disturbances it was obvious that four men arbitrarily selected could not represent all the clans in a given district. Such a small court could easily be bribed or swayed in its judgment.

Despite the crucial need to reform the Native Courts, their reorganization took longer than that of the Native Authorities. Once the Government had decided to be flexible in its approach and recognize the right of traditional leaders to rule, an *ad hoc* administration could be established as soon as these leaders had been found. Later adjustments could be made in the Native Authority. Reconstruction of the courts was more complex and in general had to wait for the completion of intelligence reports in a given district.

Nevertheless, as early as 1930 the Government began to experiment with ways of improving the courts. The most common method used throughout the two disaffected provinces was to increase the number of persons who could serve as judges. The new personnel were drawn from village leaders and heads of kindred. In a few areas, such as Aba, Bende, and Owerri divisions, some of these men were substituted for warrant chiefs. In most divisions, however, warrant chiefs were not removed; either they were ignored by the British authorities or they conformed to the new system.[42] Only in a few areas did they try to continue their domination of the courts which they had enjoyed before the disturbances.

Another change that was closely related to administrative and judicial reform was redistricting. This normally meant the transfer of a clan or part of a clan from one province to another or from one district to another. Thus in 1933 the towns of Mbala and Achara of the Isuachi clan and the entire Umuchieze clan were transferred from the Awgu Division of Onitsha Province to Owerri Province. In the same year the small Benni clan and the village of Arua were shifted to the Forcados Division of Warri Province.[43] This, however, was unusual since the provinces as constituted contained relatively homogeneous groupings. Far more common in the period of reorganization was the redrawing of court and administrative subdivisions within a division to encompass one or more clans more adequately. Correlate with this was the task of creating new Native Courts to represent clans. One of the first such creations was the new court created in October 1931 to represent approximately fifteen hundred Andoni who lived on islands in the estuary of the Imo River.[44]

Before continuing with the discussion of the reforms instituted by Cameron's administration one should note one factor that greatly complicated the process of change. Reference has been made to the worsening of the economic situation in 1929 as one cause of the women's demonstrations. The fall in prices received for oil and kernels then was only a harbinger of far worse economic distress. At the close of 1930, the price paid for oil in Calabar had fallen to approximately twelve pounds per ton and to seven pounds per ton for kernels. This represented a decrease of about 35 per cent in the course of the year.[45] But worse was yet to come. By mid-1934 the point had almost been reached where it was not worth the producer's time to gather and market palm produce. A ton of first-rate oil brought only three pounds and kernels two pounds, ten shillings at Calabar in July of that year. Fortunately this was the low point and the market began to rally in the closing months of 1934.[46] Cash sales on other products such as cotton goods, spirits, and tobacco also fell to unprecedented low levels.

In such depressed conditions, following close upon the women's disturbances, it was obvious that the Government could not expect to collect taxes at the old high rate. Tax relief was delayed partly because the authorities did not want to encourage people in the belief that the riots had caused the lowering of taxes. Nevertheless, in April 1931 there was a general reduction of taxes, amounting in some cases to 50 per cent. Where the standard rate had been seven shillings per annum for an adult male it was lowered to four shillings. In some of the more depressed areas, such as those of the Ezinihitte, Ekwerazu, and the Isuochi clans, it was even lower.[47] The Government also adopted a more lenient attitude toward payment. In December 1932, 19 per cent of the tax due was still outstanding. One year later 44 per cent of the tax had not been collected.[48] A further reduction in the tax rate to one shilling, six pence was granted in parts of Owerri Province in 1934.

Although many Native Authorities and Native Courts had been recognized by the Government before, the two acts that embodied Cameron's philosophy of native administration were approved in November 1933.[49] It should be stressed that these two ordinances were applicable to all of Nigeria and not just to the Eastern Region. In very general terms, what the new Native Authority Ordinance and Native Courts Ordinance attempted was to provide a well-reasoned, flexible framework for the functioning of local government and justice in widely different areas of Nigeria. Native authority was so defined that it could mean the highly centralized, developed form practiced in the North or the diversified and decentralized type necessary in the Eastern areas. Four separate types of Native Courts were created. The functions to be exercised by each court again varied according to the degree of organization and supposed sophistication of the society. A- and B-grade courts, or those with most power, although not so stated in the ordinance, were generally reserved for the North and West. In the East, the Clan Courts were designated C-grade and the Village Courts were D-grade.

The Clan, or C-grade courts, were those whose civil jurisdiction was limited to actions involving fifty pounds or less and criminal cases in which punishment did not exceed six months' imprisonment.[50] Each warrant constituting a court could also specify special jurisdiction of that court over cases concerning land disputes. D-grade courts were restricted to civil action concerned with cases in which the damages did not exceed twenty-five pounds and criminal action in which the maximum penalty was three months' imprisonment.[51] In some cases a C-grade court was created as a final appeal court for cases originating in a D-grade court. However, in most instances the district officer acted as the first appeal court on petition of the litigant. The Native Courts Ordinance also provided, in special cases, for appeals through the High Courts to the West African Court of Appeals.

Central to Lord Lugard's concept of teaching native peoples responsibility was the need to create native treasuries. As

has previously been discussed, the legislation affecting administration after 1919 did not, in fact, create native treasuries. There
were a few treasuries established in each province which handled
a portion of the direct tax after 1927. However, these funds
were administered by the district officers, sometimes in consultation with the warrant chiefs but more often without. Government actions after 1930 finally made possible the creation of
native treasuries. These were only in embryo form by the time
Cameron's term ended. However, the outline of their development was already clear. The direct tax formed the major source
of revenue for areas that had been gazetted Native treasuries.
By the early 1940's there would be fifty-two treasuries in
Owerri and Calabar provinces. A few of these were organized
with a finance committee whose responsibility was to prepare
the budget. In most cases, however, the district officer continued,
in consultation with the Native Authority, to prepare the estimates.[52] The depression and concomitant restriction on revenue
and the inexperienced native personnel combined to limit the
scope of the treasuries. Despite the handicaps, the people of the
East did play a large part through their own representatives in
disbursing approximately 60 per cent of the direct tax every
year.

The reforms climaxed by the twin ordinances of 1933
returned local government insofar as possible to the people. As
Lord Hailey and other commentators later noted, this decentral-
ization resulted in a very large number of native authorities and
courts which by comparison with other regions of Nigeria were
"untidy" for administrative purposes.[53] The numbers and variety
of native institutions in the East after the reorganizations were
certainly much more confusing and difficult to manage than in
1929. The system administered by Thomson and his prede-
cessors, however neat, had one great flaw. The people detested
the warrant-chief system so much that large numbers were
willing to die to change the tidy system. There were no serious
disturbances in Eastern Nigeria during and after the reforms of
Cameron despite the extreme economic pressures of the
depression.

Before 1931 this quiescence could be explained by the re-
membrance of the women's disturbances and the retribution

that followed. But memories of such events grow dim and revolt will come again if the conditions of life of the people do not improve. In the years immediately following the riots, the Government bent every effort to discover the social, legal, and political bases of the native system and to provide the people with institutions approximating the traditional. The fact that there was no serious adverse reaction to Government policies proves that the people of the East were cognizant of Cameron's aims and that they approved the results obtained.

The link between the women's disturbances in Owerri and Calabar provinces and the subsequent reforms in Nigeria seems clear, However, until the correspondence between the responsible parties is made available for research any conclusions establishing this relationship will remain speculative. With this in mind one can still state that had there been no riots, change in Government policies would have been much slower. There existed prior to December 1929 no pressure for reform. The Secretary of State depended for his knowledge of Nigerian affairs upon communications from the governor and his staff. Governor Thomson, despite numerous warnings, was satisfied that his policies were fair and that the system of local administration in the East was adequate for the "backward" peoples living there. The few days of December 1929 destroyed this complacency. People were killed, questions were asked in the House of Commons, and the Secretary of State could no longer depend upon reassurances from Lagos. At this point Lord Passfield chose as the new Governor a man of vast experience in Nigeria who had addressed himself to similar problems in Tanganyika. The choice of Cameron as Governor set the seal on the type of reform that would be instituted in Nigeria—a reform based insofar as possible upon the indigenous system of government. The tiny protest by Nyanyeruwa in Oloko, amplified by the actions of thousands of other women, showed clearly the flaws of the system created by Lugard and carried on by Clifford and Thomson. In the interest of keeping peace and administering justice, the British Government could do nothing less than tear down the old structure and attempt to construct a new one more in harmony with the desires of the people.

Appendix

A. BIOGRAPHIES OF MAJOR BRITISH ADMINISTRATORS

Compiled from Colonial Office Staff Lists
and Dictionary of National Biography

Cyril Wilson Alexander, C.M.G.
Born 1879. Educated Shrewsbury and Trinity College, Cambridge, B.A., LL.B. Assistant District Commissioner, Southern Nigeria, 1906; Junior Assistant Secretary, 1908; Acting Police Magistrate 1908. Commissioner of Lands, Lagos, 1908; 2nd-class Resident, 1919; Acting Secretary, Northern Provinces, 1924; Acting Principal Assistant Secretary, Northern Provinces, 1925; Staff grade, 1925. Acting Lt. Governor, Northern Nigeria, 1927; Lt. Governor, Southern Nigeria, 1929; Lt. Governor, Northern Nigeria, 1930.

Sir Walter Buchanan-Smith, C.M.G., M.C.
Born 1879. Educated Repton School. British North Borneo Civil Service, 1903; Assistant District Commissioner, Southern Nigeria, 1909; Acting Commissioner of Lands, Nigeria,

1912, 1914, and 1916. Attached Nigeria Regiment in Cameroons 1914–15 and in East Africa 1916–18; 1st-class District Officer, Southern Nigeria, 1918; Resident, 1921; Acting Principal Assistant Secretary, Southern Provinces, 1921, 1923, and 1925; Acting Secretary Southern Provinces, 1923 and 1925; Staff grade, 1926; Acting Lt. Governor, Southern Provinces, 1928–29 and 1930; Lt. Governor, Southern Provinces, 1930. Officer Administering Government, Nigeria, Sept.–Nov. 1930.

Sir Donald Cameron, K.C.M.G., G.B.E.
Born 1872. Educated at Rathmines School, Dublin. Entered British Guiana Civil Service, 1890. Fifth-class clerk, secretariat, 1891; 4th-class, 1895; 3rd-class and dispatch clerk, 1895; 2nd-class, 1899; private secretary to acting Governor, 1896, 1897, 1898, and 1901; Acting Assistant Governor, secretary and clerk of councils, 1900–01; Principal clerk secretariat, 1901; private secretary to Governor of Newfoundland while on leave, 1902; Assistant Colonial Secretary, Mauritius, July 1904; Acting Colonial Secretary in 1904, 1905, 1906, 1917; temporarily transferred to Southern Nigeria as Assistant Secretary, Jan., 1908; Principal Assistant Secretary, 1911; Secretary to Southern Nigeria Liquor Trade Inquiry Committee, 1909; Acting Provincial Commissioner in 1910, 1911, 1912; Acting Colonial Secretary, 27 Feb.–24 Aug., 5 Sept.–3 Oct. 1912; Deputy Governor in 1921–23; Central Secretary, Nigeria, 1 Jan. 1914; Chief Secretary to Government, 1 Jan. 1921; Acting Governor in 1921, 1923, and 1924; Governor of Tangyanika, 1924; Governor and Commander in Chief, Nigeria, 1931; Retired 1935.

Sir Hugh Clifford, G.C.M.G., G.B.E.
Born 1866; joined Perak Service, 1883; passed examination in Malay, Feb. 1885; Collector of Land Revenue, Juala Kangsar, Mar. 1885; special service to Pahang, 1887; Acting Government agent to Pahang, 1887–88; Superintendent, Ulu Pahang, 1889; Acting British Resident, Sept. 1890–Dec. 1891, and from 1893; took leading part in suppression of Pahang rebellion, 1892; Secretary to Government, Selangor, Dec. 1894 while serving as Resident to Pahang; Special Commissioner to Cocos-Keeling Island, June 1894. Led armed expedition into Trengganu and Kelantan, March–June 1895. Resident Pahang, July, 1896. Governor of North Borneo and Labuan,

1899–1901. British Resident, Pahang, 1901; Acting Colonial Secretary, Trinidad and Tobago, Sept. 1903; Colonial Secretary, Trinidad and Tobago, Sept. 1904; on deputation to British Guiana, Nov. 1905; administered Government 26 Mar.–30 Aug. 1904 and from 1 April–23 Oct. 1906; Colonial Secretary, Ceylon, May 1907; administered Government July–Aug. 1907, June–Oct. 1909, June–Nov. 1911, and 23 Nov. 1911–3 Jan. 1912. Governor of the Gold Coast, 11 Dec. 1912. Governor of Nigeria, July 1919. Governor of Ceylon, Nov. 1925; Governor of Straits Settlements and High Commissioner, Malay States, June 1927. Retired 1929.

Kenneth A. B. Cochrane
Born 1891. Educated Tonbridge School and Caius College, Cambridge. Assistant District Officer, Nigeria, 1915; Acting Resident 1932 and 1933–34; Administrative Service, Class 2, 1933.

Sir William Egerton, C.M.G.
Born 1858. Educated Tonbridge School. Cadet, Straits Settlements. Oct. 1880; Magistrate, Singapore, 1881; passed Malay, May 1882; Collector of Land Revenue, Penang, 1883; Second Magistrate of Police, Penang, May 1883; Acting Senior District Officer, Butterwork P.W., April 1890; Justice of Peace and Coroner, Straits Settlements, July 1893; Registrar of Deeds, Singapore, June 1896. Inspector of Prisons, May 1897; First Magistrate Penang, April 1897; of Singapore, Oct. 1898; Acting Colonial Secretary of State, April 1900; Acting Colonial Treasurer, Straits Settlements, Aug.–Oct. 1902; High Commissioner to Southern Nigeria, Nov. 1903.

Edward Morris Falk, A.M.I.C.E.
Born 1878. Educated at Bradford Grammar School and Victoria University. Assistant District Commissioner, Southern Nigeria, 1907; West Africa General Service medal, 1909; District Commissioner, 2nd grade, 1913. Interned as prisoner of war in Germany 1914; escaped 1915. Resumed duty in Nigeria, 1915; Resident, 1923; staff grade, 1929.

George Hugo Findlay
Born 1888. Educated Repton and Oriel College, Oxford (B.A.) Assistant District Commissioner, Nigeria, 1911; 2nd class District Officer, 1919; Assistant Secretary Southern Provinces, 1922; Class I, grade I, administrative servant, 1928. Act-

ing Administrator, Lagos, 1930. Acting Principal Secretary, 1930; Acting Secretary, Southern Provinces, 1931; staff grade, 1932; Acting Commissioner of Colony and Lands, 1934; Acting Chief Secretary, 1934.

Owen Watts Firth
Born 1884. Educated Tonbridge School. Assistant District Commissioner, Nigeria, 1911; Political Officer, Udi-Okigwi Patrol, 1915; 2nd-class District Officer, 1919; Class I, grade I, administrative servant, 1927; Acting Principal Assistant Secretary 1928.

Selwyn MacGregor Grier
Born 1878. Educated at Marlboro College and Pembroke College, Cambridge, B.A. 1900 (Classics); called to the bar, Nov. 1910. Schoolmaster at Berkhamstead, Herts, 1901–02 and at Cheam, Surrey, 1902–05. Assistant Resident, Northern Nigeria, 1906; passed in Hausa, 1907; 3rd-class Resident, Oct. 1908; in charge of Zaria Province, April 1910 and from May–Nov. 1911. Secretary for Native Affairs, Nigeria, Jan. 1921.

William Edgar Hunt, C.M.G., C.B.E.
Born 1883. Educated Warwick School and Selwyn College, Cambridge (B.A.) Assistant District Commissioner, Southern Nigeria, 1909; Assistant Colonial Secretary, Lagos, 1910; District Officer, 2nd class, 1917; Resident, 1924; staff grade, 1929; member of Commission of Inquiry into Disturbances, 1930; Acting Lt. Governor, Southern Provinces, 1930 and 1933; Commissioner of Colony and Lands, 1934.

F. H. Ingles
Born 1878. Educated at U. S. College, Newborn College, Devon and Jesus College, Cambridge, B.A. Cantab, 1902. Assistant District Commissioner, Southern Nigeria, 6 Oct. 1906; District Commissioner, 2nd grade, Feb. 1913; District Officer, 1st grade, Oct. 1919; Resident, 5 Feb. 1922 and Acting Senior Resident, Oct. 1924.

Lord Frederick John Dealtry Lugard, G.C.M.G., C.B., D.S.O.
Born 1858. Educated Rossal and Sandhurst. 1st commission, 9th Foot, May 1878; Captain, Aug. 1885; Major, Aug. 1896; Lt. Colonel, July 1899; Colonel 1905; temp. Brigadier General 1900–07. To India Sept. 1878; active service, Afghanistan,

1879–1880; Sudan, Feb.–Nov. 1885; Burma, Oct. 1886–Aug. 1887. To Africa Feb. 1888 commanding expedition against slave traders, seriously wounded. To East Africa, Nov. 1889–Oct. 1892; exploration of Sabakhi; administered Uganda. Went to Borgu to command expedition, July 1894; made treaties for Royal Niger Company and returned April 1895. Led expedition across Kalahari Desert for British Chartered Company, Feb. 1896. In Aug. 1897 appointed Commissioner and Commandant, West African Frontier Force. High Commissioner for Northern Nigeria, Dec. 1899–Sept. 1906. Governor of Hong Kong, 1 May 1907. Governor of Northern and Southern Nigeria, March 1912. Governor-General, Nigeria, 1 Jan. 1914.

Sir Claude Maxwell MacDonald, K.C.B., G.C.M.G., G.C.V.O. Born 1852. Educated at Uppingham and Sandhurst. Entered 74th Highlanders in 1872. Promoted to Major in 1882 as result of Egyptian campaign. Military attaché to Sir Evelyn Baring until 1887. Volunteer with 42nd Highlanders during Suakin expedition 1884–85. Acting agent and Consul General, Zanzibar, 1887–88. Special Commissioner to the Niger Territories, 1889. Commissioner to Berlin to delimit boundary between Oil Rivers Protectorate and the Cameroon. Appointed Commissioner and Consul General to Oil Rivers Protectorate, 1891. Retired from army 1896. Later became Minister at Peking, 1896, and was Resident there during Boxer Rebellion. Transferred to Tokyo in Oct. 1900; became Ambassador to Japan, 1905. Member of Privy Council, 1906. Retired 1912.

Sir Ralph Denham Rayment Moor, K.C.M.G. Born 1860. Educated privately. Learner in tea trade, 1880-81. Entered Royal Irish Constabulary as a cadet; rose to position of District Inspector; resigned Feb. 1891. Entered service in Nigeria under Sir Claude MacDonald, March 1891. Appointed Deputy Commissioner and Vice-Consul in Oil Rivers Protectorate and adjoining native territory, July 1892; acting administrator and Consul General, Aug. 1892–Feb. 1893, April 1894–Nov. 1894, and July–Dec. 1895; appointed Consul in Jan. 1896. Commissioner and Consul General, Niger Coast Protectorate and adjoining native territories; Consul in Cam-

eroons and to Fernando Po in Jan. 1896. Appointed High
Commissioner for Southern Nigeria, 1900. Retired because
of health Oct. 1903.

Lt. Col. Harry Claude Moorhouse, C.M.G., D.S.O., officer of
Legion of Honor.
Entered Royal Artillery, 1891; Captain, 1899; Major, 1902,
temporary Lt. Colonel, 1914. Served in Uganda 1898; West
Africa, 1900; Southern Nigeria, 1901–02, Northern Nigeria,
1903; Southern Nigeria, 1904 (D.S.O.). Chief Assistant-Colo-
nial Secretary, Southern Nigeria, 1908; Secretary Southern
Provinces, 1 Jan. 1914; Lt. Governor, Nigeria, 1 Jan. 1920.

Sir Herbert Richmond Palmer C.M.G., C.B.E.
Educated Oundle School and Trinity Hall, Cambridge, M.A.,
LL.B., Barrister-at-law, Middle Temple 1904; Assistant Resi-
dent, Northern Nigeria, Oct. 1904; Commissioner of Native
Revenue, Northern Nigeria, 1911, revenue mission to Anglo-
Egyptian Sudan 1912; supervisor, native revenue, Nigeria,
1914; Acting Resident Kano Province, 1915–16; Resident,
Bornu Province, 1917; visited the Anglo-Egyptian Sudan from
Bornu via Wadai and Darfur, 1918; Acting Lt. Governor,
Northern Nigeria, May–Dec. 1921; Acting Resident Sokoto
Province, April–May 1922. Lt. Governor, Northern Nigeria,
May 1925; Governor of Gambia, 1930.

Major Upton Fitzherbert Ruxton, C.M.G.
Born 1873, Assistant Resident, Nigeria, Feb. 1901; 2nd-class
Resident, Oct. 1902; 1st-class Resident, Oct. 1908; Seconded
to Admiralty April 1916 to May 1919; seconded to Foreign
Office for Political Duties, Constantinople, May 1919, and
returned to Nigeria Aug. 1921; Lt. Governor, Southern Provinces, Oct. 1925–March 1929.

Sir Graeme Thomson, K.C.M.G.
Born 1875, educated Winchester and New College, Oxford;
higher division clerk in Admiralty, 1900; Assistant Director
of Transport, 1914; Director of Transport, 1914; Colonial
Secretary of Ceylon, Sept. 1919; Officer administrating Gov-
ernment, 8–18 Jan. 1920 and Mar.–Sept. 1920; Governor and
Commander in Chief, British Guiana, 1923; Governor and
Commander in Chief, Nigeria, 1925.

George John Frederick Tomlinson
B.A. Oxford, Barrister-at-law, Inner Temple. Served in edu-

cation department, Transvaal, Feb. 1903–Oct. 1904. Assistant Resident Northern Nigeria, July 1907; seconded to Gold Coast as Director of Education, Dec. 1909–Dec. 1910; 3rd-class Resident, Northern Nigeria, April 1911. Assistant Secretary for Native Affairs, Nigeria, Jan. 1921.

B. BIBLIOGRAPHY

Documents

British Government Correspondence
  Foreign Office Files
    F.O. 2/63
    F.O. 2/64
    F.O. 2/83
    F.O. 2/120
    F.O. 2/121
    F.O. 2/179
    F.O. 2/180
    F.O. 84/1940
  Colonial Office Files
    C.O. 380/152
    C.O. 520/7
    C.O. 520/8
    C.O. 520/10
    C.O. 520/13
    C.O. 520/14
    C.O. 520/15
    C.O. 520/18
    C.O. 520/29
    C.O. 520/31
    C.O. 583/9
    C.O. 583/10
    C.O. 583/11
    C.O. 588/1
    C.O. 592/2
    C.O. 592/3
    C.O. 657/24
    C.O. 657/27
Federal Archives, Ibadan, Nigeria
  Annual Reports

M

Calabar Province
  C.S.O. 26/3, File 11929
    Vol. 6, 1928
    Vol. 7, 1929
    Vol. 8, 1930
    Vol. 9, 1931
    Vol. 12, 1934
  C.S.O. 26/2, File 11930
    Vol. 6, 1928
    Vol. 7, 1929
    Vol. 8, 1930
    Vol. 9, 1931
    Vol. 10, 1932
    Vol. 11, 1933
    Vol. 12, 1934
Assessment and Reassessment Reports
  Calabar Province
    C.S.O. 26/2
      File 20677, Opobo Division, 1927
      File 20682, Uyo District, 1927
      File 20689, Calabar Division, 1927
      File 20690, Aro District, 1927
  Owerri Province
    Chief Secretary's Office (C.S.O.) 26/2
      File 20610/4, Aba Native Court Area, 1927
      File 20610/6, Asa Native Court Area, 1927
      File 20621, Degema Division, 1927
      File 20634, Ahoada Division, 1927
      File 20645, Okigwi District, Okigwi Division, 1927
      File 20646, Bende Division, 1927
  Calabar Province
    C.S.O. 26/3
      File 26994, Andoni People, Andoni Native Court, Opobo Division, 1931
      File 27627, Vol. 1 and 2, Efik, Qua [Kwa] and Efut Peoples, Calabar Division, 1932 and 1933
      File 29017, Aro Clan, Aro-Chuku Division, 1933
    Eastern Provinces (E.P.) 3759, Native Authority Ordinance, 1916
Intelligence Reports

Owerri Province
C.S.O. 26/4
File 28239, Abua Clan, Ahoada Division, 1932
File 28939, Abam Clan, Bende Division, 1933
File 30984, Alayi Clan, Bende Division, 1934
File 31016, Akassa Clan, Degema Division, 1935
Owerri Province (O.W.) 225/14, Memorandum by
Lugard on Native Courts
O.W. 104/14, Circular Memorandum #5
Government Publications
Great Britain, House of Commons, Papers by Command
C 7596
C 7638
C 7977
C 8677
C 9375
Cmd. 468
Cmd. 2744
Cmd. 3784
Miscellaneous
Sir Donald Cameron, *Principles of Native Administration
and Their Application* (Lagos: 1934)
S.M. Grier, *Report on the Eastern Provinces by the Sec-
retary for Native Affairs* (Lagos: 1922)
Lord Hailey, *Native Administration in British African
Territories*, 5 Vols. (London: 1951)
Sir Edward Hertslet, *Map of Africa by Treaty*, 3 Vols.
(London: 1909)
Lord Lugard, Political Memoranda (Lagos: 1918)
C. K. Meek, *An Ethnographic Report upon the Peoples of
Nsukka Division, Onitsha Province* (Lagos: 1933)
————*Report on Social and Political Organization in the
Owerri Division* (Lagos: 1934)
G. J. F. Tomlinson, *Report of a Tour in the Eastern Prov-
inces by the Assistant Secretary for Native Affairs*
(Lagos: 1923)
Nigeria
Annual Reports, 1925–1935
Authenticated Ordinances, 1901–1935
Legislative Council, *Sessional Paper #12, Report of a Com-*

mission of Enquiry Appointed to Inquire into Certain Incidents at Opobo, Abak, and Utu-Ekpo in December 1929

Legislative Council, *Sessional Paper #28, Report of a Commission of Enquiry Appointed to Inquire into the Disturbances in Calabar and Owerri Provinces, December 1929*

Books

J. F. Ade Ajayi, *Christian Missions in Nigeria, 1841–1891* (Evanston, Ill.: 1965)

Ebiegberi Joe Alagoa, *The Small Brave City–State* (Madison: Wis.: 1964)

J. C. Anene, *Southern Nigeria in Transition, 1885–1906* (Cambridge: 1966)

William Baikie, *Narrative of an Exploring Voyage up the Kw'ora and Binne in 1854* (London: 1856)

R. L. Buell, *The Native Problem in Africa,* 2 Vols. (New York: 1928)

Sir Alan C. Burns, *History of Nigeria* (New York: 1963)

Sir Donald Cameron, *My Tanganyika Experience and Some Nigeria* (London: 1939)

L. T. Chubb, *Ibo Land Tenure* (Ibadan: 1961)

J. S. Coleman, *Nigeria: Background to Nationalism* (Berkeley, Calif.: 1958)

Michael Crowder, *A Short History of Nigeria* (New York: 1966)

Basil Davidson, *Black Mother* (London: 1961)

Harm J. De Blij, *A Geography of Subsaharan Africa* (Chicago: 1964)

K. Onwuka Dike, *Origins of the Niger Mission, 1841–1891* (Lagos: 1957)

———, *Trade and Politics in the Niger Delta, 1830–1855* (Oxford: 1956)

J. U. Egharevba, *A Short History of Benin* (Ibadan: 1960)

John Flint, *Sir George Goldie and the Making of Nigeria* (London: 1960)

Daryll Forde, ed., *Efik Traders of Old Calabar* (London: 1956)

———, and G. I. Jones, *The Ibo and Ibibio Speaking Peoples of South-Eastern Nigeria* (London: 1962)

W. N. M. Geary, *Nigeria Under British Rule* (New York: 1965)

M. M. Green, *Ibo Village Affairs* (New York: 1964)

Lord Hailey, *An African Survey* (London: 1945)

G. I. Jones, *The Trading States of the Oil Rivers* (London: 1963)

Mary Kingsley, *West African Studies* (London: 1899)

Sylvia Leith-Ross, *African Women* (New York: 1965)

A. G. Leonard, *The Lower Niger and Its Tribes* (London: 1906)

Christopher Lloyd, *The Navy and the Slave Trade* (London: 1949)

Lord Lugard, *The Diaries of Lord Lugard*, Vol. 4 (Evanston, Ill.: 1963)

————, *The Dual Mandate* (London: 1963)

Daniel P. Mannix and Malcolm Cowley, *Black Cargoes* (New York: 1962)

C. K. Meek, *Land, Law and Custom in the Colonies* (London: 1946)

————, *Law and Authority in a Nigerian Tribe* (London: 1937)

S. N. Chinwuba Obi, *The Ibo Law of Property* (London: 1963)

Margery Perham, *Lugard: The Years of Adventure, 1858–1898* (London: 1956)

————, *Lugard: The Years of Authority, 1898–1945* (London: 1960)

————, *Native Administration in Nigeria* (London: 1937)

L. Dudley Stamp, *Africa, A Study of Tropical Development* (New York: 1957)

P. Amaury Talbot, *The Peoples of Southern Nigeria*, Vol. 1, Historical Notes (London: 1926)

Victor Uchendu, *The Igbo of Southeast Nigeria* (New York: 1965)

Articles

A. E. Afigbo, "Oral Tradition and History in Eastern Nigeria," Parts I, II, *African Notes*, April, October 1966

J. F. Ade Ajayi, "The British Occupation of Lagos, 1851–61," *Nigeria Magazine*, No. 69 (August 1961)

Ebiegberi Joe Alagoa, "Oral Tradition Among the Ijo [Ijaw] of the Niger Delta," *Journal of African History*, Vol. 7, No. 3

J. C. Anene, "The Southern Nigeria Protectorate and the Aros, 1900–1902," *Journal of the Historical Society of Nigeria*, December 1956

A. F. B. Bridges, "The Oil Palm Industry in Nigeria," *Farm and Forest*, January–June 1946

Sir Donald Cameron, "Native Administration in Nigeria and Tanganyika," *Journal of the Royal African Society*, 30, Vol. 36, November 1937

A. J. Udo Ema, "The Ekpe Society," *Nigeria*, Vol. 16

J. Harris, "Some Aspects of the Economics of Sixteen Ibo Individuals," *Africa*, Vol, 14, No. 6

W. R. G. Horton, "The Ohu System of Slavery in a Northern Ibo Village Group, *Africa*, Vol. 24, No. 4

G. I. Jones "Ibo Land Tenure," *Africa*, Vol. 19, No. 4

———, "Who are the Aro?" *Nigerian Field*, Vol. 8 (1939)

Sylvia Leith-Ross, "Notes on the Osu System Among the Ibo of Owerri Province, Nigeria," *Africa*, Vol. 10

H. K. Offrony "Age Grades, Their Power and Influence in Village Life," *West African Review*, December 1948

———, "The Ibo Peoples," *West African Review*, February 1947

Simon Ottenberg, "Ibo Oracles of Intergroup Relations," *Southwestern Journal of Anthropology*, Vol. 14, No. 3

Margery Perham, "Some Problems of Indirect Rule in Africa," *Journal of the Royal Society of Arts*, May 18, 1934

Unpublished Sources

A. E. Afigbo, "The Era of the Warrant Chiefs in Eastern Nigeria," Ph.D. thesis, University of Ibadan, 1964

S. M. (Tekana) Tamuno, "The Development of British Administrative Control of Southern Nigeria, 1900–1912," Ph.D. Thesis, University of London, 1963

Notes

For the following abbreviations, see full references in the first section of the Bibliography, *Documents*, under the following headings:

C	*Government Publications, Great Britain*
Cmd.	*Government Publications, Great Britain*
C.O.	*British Government Correspondence*
C.S.O.	*Federal Archives, Ibadan, Nigeria*
F.O.	*British Government Correspondence*
Sessional	*Government Publications, Nigeria, Legislative Council*

I: THE LAND AND THE PEOPLE

1. For a brief, informative account of the geography of Eastern Nigeria, see Harm de Blij, *A Geography of Subsaharan Africa* (Chicago: 1964), pp. 324–6 and 335–8.

2. Daryll Forde and G. I. Jones, *The Ibo and Ibibio Speaking Peoples of South-Eastern Nigeria* (London: 1962), p. 13.

3. *Ibid.*, pp. 13–14.

4. C.S.O. 26/2, File 11930, Vol. 8, 1930, p. 2.

5. For a detailed analysis of the Ijaw, see P. A. Talbot, *Peoples of Southern Nigeria* (London: 1926), Vol. 1, and A. G. Leonard, *The Lower Niger and Its Tribes* (London: 1906).

6. G. I. Jones, *The Trading States of the Oil Rivers* (London: 1963), pp. 177–8 and C.S.O. 26/2, File 11930, Vol. 9, p. 11.

7. An excellent analysis of the house system in the nineteenth century, written by Comte C. de Cardi, is "The House System in the Brass River Area," Appendix I, in Mary Kingsley, *West African Studies* (London: 1899), pp. 475 ff. See also Jones, *op. cit.*, pp. 51–62.

8. *Ibid.*, *West African Studies*, p. 477.

9. Daryll Forde, ed., *Efik Traders of Old Calabar* (London: 1956).

10. Forde and Jones, *op. cit.*, pp. 79–81.

11. *Ibid.*, pp. 81–3.

12. *Ibid.*, pp. 87–8.

13. *Ibid.*, pp. 86–7.

14. *Ibid.*, pp. 85–6.

15. *Ibid.*, pp. 89–92 and C.S.O. 26/2, File 11929, Vol. 9, 1931, pp. 7–9.

16. Forde and Jones, *op. cit.*, pp. 71–2.

17. *Ibid.*, p. 73.

18. *Ibid.*, pp. 73–4.

19. *Ibid.*, pp. 71–2.

20. S. N. Chinwuba Obi, *The Ibo Law of Property* (London: 1963), p. 2.

21. *Ibid.*, pp. 2–3.

22. Forde and Jones, *op. cit.*, pp. 11–12.

23. Obi, *op. cit.*, pp. 17–18.

24. *Ibid.*, p. 17.

25. *Ibid.*, pp. 15–16.

26. Ibid., pp. 13–15 and Victor Uchendu, *The Igbo of Southeast Nigeria* (New York: 1965), pp. 41–3.

27. Obi, *op. cit.*, pp. 12–13.

28. M. M. Green, *Ibo Village Affairs* (New York: 1964), p. 7.

29. Uchendu, *op. cit.*, pp. 86–8.

30. Green, *op. cit.*, pp. 44–5. For the influence of the women's Ogbo society among the Ibo, see Memo by C. T. Lawrence, Secretary, Southern Provinces, Annexare I, Nigerian Government, Legislative Council, *Sessional Paper #28*, pp. 4–5.

31. W. R. G. Horton, "The Ohu System of Slavery in a Northern Ibo Village Group," *Africa*, Vol. 24, No. 4, and Green, *op. cit.*, p. 23.

32. Green, *op. cit.*, p. 24.

33. G. I. Jones, "Ibo Land Tenure," *Africa*, Vol. 19, No. 4, pp. 309–23.

34. Sylvia Leith-Ross, *African Women* (New York: 1965), pp. 63–5.

35. *Ibid.*, pp. 338–46, and Uchendu, *op. cit.*, pp. 27–30.

36. Uchendu, *op. cit.*, p. 26.

37. C.S.O. 26/3, File No. 29017, Intelligence Report on the Aro Clan, Calabar Province. See also Simon Ottenberg, "Ibo Oracles and Inter-group Relations," *Southwestern Journal of Anthropology*, Vol. 14, No. 3, pp. 295–307.

38. The best description of the Aro is in the Intelligence Report compiled in 1933 by Assistant District Officer T. M. Shankland, C.S.O. 26/3, File 29017. See also G. I. Jones, "Who Are the Aro?" *Nigerian Field*, No. 3, 1939.

II: THE GROWTH OF BRITISH INFLUENCE

1. G. I. Jones, *The Trading States of the Oil Rivers* (London: 1963), pp. 9–11, 177–80.

2. *Ibid.*, pp. 57–61, 190.

3. *Ibid.*, pp. 55–7.

4. C.S.O. 26/3, File 29017.

5. K. Onwuka Dike, *Trade and Politics in the Niger Delta, 1830–1855* (Oxford: 1956), pp. 7–8.

6. For a full discussion of the suppression of the slave trade, see Christopher Lloyd, *The Navy and the Slave Trade* (London: 1949) and Daniel Mannix and Malcolm Cowley, *Black Cargoes* (New York: 1962).

7. Dike, *op. cit.*, pp. 65–80.

8. *Ibid.*, p. 99.

9. *Ibid.*, pp. 60–1.

10. Michael Crowder, *A Short History of Nigeria* (New York: 1966), p. 158.

11. Dike, *op. cit.*, pp. 128–46.

12. *Ibid.*, p. 176, and J. F. Ade Ajayi, "The British Occupation of Lagos, 1851–61," *Nigeria Magazine*, No. 69 (August 1961).

13. William Baikie, *Narrative of an Exploring Voyage up the Rivers Kw'ora and Binne in 1854* (London: 1856).

14. Dike, *op. cit.*, pp. 169–71.

15. For fuller treatment of missionary activity in this period, see J. F. Ade Ajayi, *Christian Missions in Nigeria, 1841–1891* (Evanston, Ill.: 1965).

16. J. C. Anene, *Southern Nigeria in Transition, 1885–1906* (Cambridge: 1966), pp. 42–5.

17. *Ibid.*, pp. 151–2.

18. Ebiegberi Joe Alagoa, *The Small Brave City-State* (Madison, Wis.: 1964).

19. Great Britain, House of Commons, Parliamentary Papers, V (412), *Report of the Select Committee on State of British Settlements on the West Coast of Africa, 1865.*

N

20. John Flint, *Sir George Goldie and the Making of Nigeria* (London: 1960).

21. For Charter to National African Company, see C.O. 380/152, and Sir Edward Hertslet, *Map of Africa by Treaty*, 3 Vols. (London: 1909), Vol. 1, p. 446. For Declaration of the British Protectorate in 1887, see p. 449.

22. Hertslet, Vol. 1, p. 445.

23. Anene, *op. cit.*, pp. 81–91.

24. Flint, *op. cit.*, pp. 216–63.

25. Anene, *op. cit.*, pp. 135–6.

26. Crowder, *op. cit.*, pp. 199–200.

27. Anene, *op. cit.*, pp. 151–61.

28. Alagoa, *op .cit.*, pp. 91–126.

29. Egharevba, *A Short History of Benin* (Ibadan: 1960), pp. 50–61.

30. Major MacDonald was knighted in 1893.

31. For a more detailed comment on MacDonald, see Anene, *op. cit.*, pp. 162–3.

32. *Ibid.*, pp. 184–6.

33. On the revocation of the Charter, see C 9372. For Order in Council, 27 December 1899 and Royal Instructions, see C.O. 380/152.

34. Anene, *op. cit.*, pp. 203–22. The number of towns in Kwa Ibo at this time is open to question.

35. C.S.O. 26/3, File 29017.

36. Details of the Aro Expedition are in C.O. 520/10. See also Moor's Memorandum dated 24 April 1902 in C.O. 520/13.

37. Anene, *op. cit.*, p. 231.

38. Moor to Colonial Office, 12 April 1902, C.O. 520/14.

39. C.O. 520/15 and C.O. 520/18.

40. C.O. 520/18.

41. C.O. 520/31.

42. *Ibid.*

III: THE ESTABLISHMENT OF BRITISH CONTROL

1. Foreign Office to MacDonald, 17 January 1889, F.O. 84/1940.

2. *Ibid.*, Confidential Report, MacDonald to Salisbury, 12 June 1889.

3. J. C. Anene, *Southern Nigeria in Transition, 1885–1906* (Cambridge, 1966, p. 139. For details of MacDonald's administration, see C 7596, *Report on the Administration of the Niger Coast Protectorate, 1891–1894*.

4. A. E. Afigbo, "The Era of the Warrant Chiefs in Eastern Nigeria," unpublished Ph.D. thesis, University of Ibadan, 1964, p. 65.

5. Anene, *op. cit.*, p. 203.

6. *Ibid.*, p. 255.

7. C.O. 588/1.

8. *Ibid.*

9. Native House Rule Proclamation #26, 1901, C.O. 520/10.

10. Order in Council, 27 December 1899, C.O. 520/1.

11. C.O. 380/152.
12. Moor to Colonial Office, 14 December 1901, C.O. 520/10.
13. S. M. (Tekana) Tamuno, "The Development of British Administrative Control of Southern Nigeria, 1900–1912," unpublished Ph.D. Thesis, University of London, 1963, p. 83.
14. *Ibid.*, p. 84.
15. The Police Proclamation #4, 1902, C.O. 588/1.
16. See Moor to Colonial Office, 8 August 1902, C.O. 520/15.
17. Native Courts Proclamation #9, 1900, C.O. 588/1.
18. Native Courts Proclamation #25, 1901, C.O. 588/1.
19. Afigbo, *op. cit.*, pp. 115–6.
20. Supreme Court Proclamation #6, 1900, and Commissioners' Proclamation #8, 1900, C.O. 588/1.
21. Probyn to Colonial Office, 9 August 1901, C.O. 520/8.
22. Tamuno, *op. cit.*, p. 100.
23. Moor to Colonial Office, 7 January 1903, C.O. 520/18.
24. Tamuno, *op. cit.*, p. 227.
25. *Sessional Paper* #5, 1906, C.O. 592/2.
26. Native Courts Proclamation #7, 1906, C.O. 588/1.
27. Afigbo, *op. cit.*, pp. 93–4.
28. *Ibid.*, pp. 76–92.
29. *Ibid.*, p. 97.
30. *Ibid.*, p. 131.
31. *Ibid.*, pp. 129–30.
32. C.O. 592/3.
33. Afigbo, *op. cit.*, p. 134.
34. *Ibid.*, p. 136.
35. *Ibid.*
36. For example, in 1905, £60,000 was diverted from the South to meet northern expenditures. C.O. 520/29.
37. F. D. Lugard, *Amalgamation of Northern and Southern Nigeria and Administration, 1912–1919*, Cmd. 468.
38. Margery Perham, *Lugard: The Years of Adventure, 1858–1898* (London: 1956), p. 414.
39. C.O. 583/9.
40. Lugard is very candid in his opinions expressed in Cmd. 468, p. 21. See also his speech before Legislative Council, 12 March 1914, in C.O. 583/11.
41. Cmd. 468, p. 21. Emphasis mine.
42. Native Courts Ordinance #8, 1914, *Nigeria Gazette*, Jan. 1914.
43. Provincial Courts Ordinance #3, 1914, C.O. 583/10.
44. Cmd. 468, p. 21.
45. Afigbo, *op. cit.*, p. 160.
46. Owerri Provincial Files, 225/14.
47. Native Authority Ordinance, 1916, Eastern Province Files, 3759.
48. *Ibid.*
49. *Ibid.* and *Nigeria Gazette*, 1917, p. 353.
50. Afigbo, *op. cit.*, p. 168.
51. *Ibid.*, p. 174.

52. S. M. Grier, *Report on the Eastern Provinces by the Secretary for Native Affairs* (Lagos: 1922).

53. G. J. F. Tomlinson, *Report of a Tour in the Eastern Provinces by the Assistant Secretary for Native Affairs* (Lagos: 1923).

54. *Ibid.*, p. 5.

55. For example see C.S.O. 26/2, File 20634 Owerri Province, Ahoada Division; File 20645 Okigwi Division; File 20621, Degema Division; File 20646 Bende Division.

IV: THE DECISION TO TAX

1. Lugard to Harcourt, 10 August 1914, C.S.O. 9/1/8.

2. "Notes on Taxation in Southern Provinces" by Lugard, 13 March 1915, *Ibid.*

3. Lugard to Harcourt, 10 August 1914, *Ibid.*

4. Harcourt to Lugard, 14 August 1914, *Ibid.*

5. "Notes on Taxation in Southern Provinces" by Lugard, 13 March 1915, *Ibid.*

6. *Ibid.*

7. Harcourt to Lugard, 30 April 1915, *Ibid.*

8. A. E. Afigbo, "The Era of the Warrant Chiefs in Eastern Nigeria," unpublished Ph.D. Thesis, University of Ibadan, 1964, p. 183.

9. *Ibid.*, pp. 184–6.

10. S. M. Grier, *Report on the Eastern Provinces by the Secretary for Native Affairs* (Lagos: 1922).

11. G. J. F. Tomlinson, *Report of a tour in the Eastern Provinces by the Assistant Secretary for Native Affairs* (Lagos: 1923).

12. C.S.O. 26/2, File 17720, Vol. 1, p. 3.

13. Minute by Thomson, 11 November 1925, *Ibid.*, p. 2.

14. Circular of Acting Lieutenant-Governor, 2 December 1925, *Ibid.*, p. 3.

15. *Ibid.*, pp. 73–4.

16. *Ibid.*, pp. 91–4.

17. *Ibid.*, pp. 81–7.

18. Minute by Ruxton, 4 October 1926, *Ibid.*, p. 6.

19. Draft Tax Ordinance, *Ibid.*, pp. 19–23.

20. Palmer to Ruxton, 2 October 1926, *Ibid.*, pp. 108–12.

21. Minute by Alexander, 29 September 1926, *Ibid.*, pp. 115–9.

22. Minute by Tomlinson, 5 November 1926, *Ibid.*, pp. 136–48.

23. *Ibid.*, p. 140. Emphasis mine.

24. Minute by Ruxton, 4 October 1926, *Ibid.*, pp. 4–5.

25. Memorandum by Thomson, 18 November 1926, C.S.O. 26/2, File 17720, Vol. 2, p. 193.

26. Draft Amendment Ordinance, *Ibid.*, p. 172.

27. Memo by Thomson, 18 November 1926, *Ibid.*, p. 194.

28. *Nigeria Gazette*, 10 March 1927.

29. Appendix X, C.S.O. 26/2, File 17720, Vol. 2.

30. *Ibid.*, p. 212.

31. *Ibid.*, p. 257.

32. *Sessional* #28, p. 4.

33. Amery to Thomson, 24 January 1927, C.S.O. 26/2, File 17720, Vol. 2.

34. C.S.O. 26/2, File 20646, p. 11.

35. Letter Chief Secretary to Lieutenant-Governor, Southern Provinces 9 April 1927, C.S.O. 26/2, File 18417, Vol. 1, p. 19.

36. Hunt's Report, 19 May 1927, *Ibid.*, pp. 20–35 see note 35.

37. *Ibid.*, p. 34.

38. C.S.O. 26/2, File 20646, p. 42.

39. C.S.O. 26/2, File 20645, pp. 6–7.

40. C.S.O. 26/2, File 20621, p. 8.

41. *Ibid.*, pp. 88–9.

42. C.S.O. 26/2, File 20610/4, p. 7.

43. C.S.O. 26/2, File 20610/6, p. 15.

44. C.S.O. 26/2, File 18417, Vol. 1, p. 52.

45. C.S.O. 26/2, File 20646, p. 17.

46. *Ibid.*

47. C.S.O. 26/2, File 20610/6.

48. *Ibid.*, p. 16.

49. *Ibid.*

50. C.S.O. 26/2, File 20610/4, pp. 9–10.

51. C.S.O. 26/2, File 18417, Vol. 1, p. 51.

52. *Ibid.*, p. 52.

53. Annual Report, *Southern Provinces*, 1927, pp. 75–7.

54. Letter Lieutenant-Governor to "My Dear John," 2 August 1927, in C.S.O. 26/2, File 18417, Vol. 1, pp. 72–5.

55. C.S.O. 26/2, File 20645, p. 45.

56. C.S.O. 26/2, File 20610/4, pp. 14–17.

57. C.S.O. 26/2, File 20646, p. 19.

58. *Ibid.*, p. 52.

59. C.S.O. 26/2, File 20621, p. 90.

60. C.S.O. 26/2, File 20646, p. 3.

61. *Ibid.*, p. 52.

62. *Ibid.*, p. 26.

63. C.S.O. 26/2, File 18417, Vol. 1, p. 79.

64. *Ibid.*, pp. 79–81.

65. *Annual Report, Southern Provinces*, 1929, p. 33.

66. *Ibid.*, p. 45.

67. *Ibid.*, p. 4.

68. C.O. 657/24.

69. *Annual Police Report, Southern Provinces*, 1930, p. 7.

V: THE BEGINNING OF THE DISTURBANCES

1. Compiled from *Sessional #28*, pp. 38, 102.

2. *Ibid.*, p. 104.

3. *Ibid.*, p. 104.

4. *Ibid.*, p. 103.

5. M. M. Green, *Ibo Village Affairs* (New York: 1964), pp. 37–39.

6. Daryll Forde and G. I. Jones, *The Ibo and Ibibio Speaking Peoples of South-Eastern Nigeria* (London: 1962), p. 73.

7. Green, *op. cit.*, p. 215.

8. *Ibid.*, p. 215.

9. *Ibid.*, pp. 217–30.

10. Report by Captain J. N. Hill, D. O. Bende, in Memo by C. T. Lawrence, Sec., Southern Provinces, *Sessional #28*, Annexare I, p. 4.

11. *Ibid.*, p. 5.

12. Nigerian Government. Legislative Council, *Sessional #12*, Minutes of Evidence, p. 20.

13. Lawrence's Memo, *Sessional #28*, p. 11.

14. *Ibid.*, pp. 11–12.

15. *Ibid.*, pp. 12–13.

16. *Annual Report, Southern Provinces*, 1928, p. 33.

17. *Sessional #28*, p. 114.

18. C.S.O. 26/2, File No. 20646, p. 17.

19. The events at Oloko and Bende taken from *Sessional #28*, pp. 11–16. See also Appendix V for time scale of events.

20. In most Ibo areas there is a four-day week. The days are Eke, Orie, Afo, and Nkwo. Markets are held in different villages on specific days. Thus Orie was the day assigned to Oloko for trading.

21. *Sessional #28*, p. 15.

22. *Ibid.*, footnote p. 15.

23. The Umuahia affair is related in *ibid.*, p. 20.

24. *Ibid.*, p. 18.

25. *Ibid.*, p. 55.

VI: THE SPREAD OF THE REVOLT

1. *Sessional #28*, p. 18.

2. *Ibid.*, p. 36.

3. *Ibid.*, Appendix V.

4. *Ibid.*, Appendix V.

5. For details of events at Aba, see *Ibid.*, Appendix V and pp. 44–47.

6. *Ibid.*, pp. 45–46.

7. *Ibid.*, p. 46.

8. *Ibid.*, Appendix V.

9. For time scale of events in Owerri town, see *Ibid.*, Appendix V.

10. *Ibid.*, Appendix V.

11. The most concise report of troubles in Abak are in Sessional *#12*, pp. 8–14. Also *Ibid.*, pp. 62–71.

12. The first Commission's reports of casualties were too low. The later Commission's report estimates are in all probability accurate. See *Sessional #28*, p. 71.

13. Events at Opobo are detailed in *Sessional #12*, pp. 3–8 and *Sessional #28*, pp. 73–87.

14. *Sessional #12*, Appendix A.

15. *Sessional #28*, p. 87.
16. *Ibid.*, Appendix V.
17. *Sessional #12*, Minutes of Evidence, p. 10.
18. *Sessional #28*, Minutes of Evidence, p. 17.
19. *Ibid.*, p. 105.
20. *Sessional #12*, p. 6.
21. *Sessional #28*, p. 105.
22. *Sessional #12*, Minutes of Evidence, p. 11.
23. *Ibid.*, p. 10.
24. *Sessional #28*, p. 20.
25. *Ibid.*, p. 20.
26. *Ibid.*, p. 20.
27. *Sessional #12*, Minutes of Evidence, p. 43.
28. C.S.O. 26/2, File No. 11930, Vol. 8, 1930, p. 9.

VII: THE GOVERNMENT'S REACTION

1. *Peace Preservation.Ordinance #15*, 1917.
2. *Collective Punishment Ordinance #20*, 1915.
3. C.O. 657/24, p. 49.
4. *Sessional #28*, pp. 118–20.
5. *Ibid.*, p. 120.
6. *Ibid.*, Appendix V.
7. *Ibid.*, p. 120.
8. C.O. 657/27, pp. 9–10.
9. C.S.O. 26/2, File No. 11930, Vol. 8, 1930, pp. 8, 41–42.
10. For examples of questions asked, see Great Britain, House of Commons, *Parliamentary Debates* (5th Series), Vol. 233, Col. 1392–93 and Vol. 238, Col. 952.
11. *Sessional #12*.
12. *Sessional #28*.
13. *Ibid.*, pp. 127–32.
14. *Ibid.*, p. 130.
15. *Ibid.*, p. 128.
16. *Ibid.*, p. 128.
17. *Ibid.*, pp. 125–26.
18. *Legislative Council Minutes*, 9th Session, 1931, pp. 36–57.
19. Cmd. 3784, *Despatch from the Secretary of State . . . regarding the Commission of Inquiry into the Disturbances at Aba and Other Places*, February 1931.
20. *Ibid.*, p. 4.
21. *Ibid.*, p. 5.
22. *Ibid.*, p. 4.
23. Memorandum by C. T. Lawrence in *Sessional #28*, p. 9.
24. *Ibid.*, p. 9.
25. *Ibid.*, pp. 9–10.
26. C.O. 657/27, p. 9. An interesting commentary on the suspicious attitude toward anthropologists held by the Colonial Office can be seen

in the discussion following a paper on Nigeria read by Margery Perham in 1934. See "Some Problems of Indirect Rule in Africa," *Journal of the Royal Society of Arts*, May 18, 1934.

27. C. K. Meek, *An Ethnographic Report upon the Peoples of Nsukka Division, Onitsha Province* (Lagos: 1933) and *Report on Social and Political Organization in the Owerri Division* (Lagos: 1934).

28. *Colonial Office Reports, Annual, Nigeria*, 1933, p. 7.

29. The best statement of Cameron's views is to be found in his *Principles of Native Administration and Their Application* (Lagos: 1934).

30. Sir Donald Cameron, *My Tanganyika Service and Some Nigeria* (London: 1939), p. 278.

31. "Native Administration in Nigeria and Tanganyika," *Journal of the Royal African Society*, Vol. 36, November 30, 1937, p. 4.

32. *Ibid.*, p. 11.

33. *Ibid.*, p. 10.

34. C.S.O. 26/2, File No. 11930, Vol. 10, 1932, pp. 5–6.

35. *Ibid.*, p. 9.

36. C.S.O. 26/2, File No. 11929, Vol. 9, 1931, p. 11.

37. C.S.O. 26/3, File No. 27627, Vol. 1, p. 25.

38. Margery Perham, *Native Administration in Nigeria* (London: 1937), p. 246.

39. See map in Appendix of C.S.O. 26/2, File No. 11929, Vol. 12, 1934.

40. Covering letter by Senior Resident Findley, October 10, 1933, in C.S.O. 26/3, File No. 27627, Vol. 2.

41. C.S.O. 26/2, File No. 11930, Vol. 9, 1931, pp. 19–20.

42. *Ibid.*, p. 20.

43. C.S.O. 26, File No. 11930, Vol. 11, 1933, p. 4.

44. C.S.O. 26/3, File No. 26994. For final approval, see Minute Paper by Secretary of Southern Provinces, April 4, 1933.

45. C.S.O. 26/2, File No. 11930, Vol. 8, 1930, p. 65.

46. C.S.O. 26/2, File No. 11929, Vol. 12, 1934, p. 7.

47. C.S.O. 26/2, File No. 11930, Vol. 11, 1933, p. 13.

48. *Ibid.*, p. 14.

49. *Native Authority Ordinance No. 43*, 1933, and *Native Courts Ordinance No. 44*, 1933.

50. In cases of livestock theft the punishment could be a maximum of twelve months' imprisonment, twelve strokes, or a fine of ten pounds.

51. In cases of livestock theft the punishment could be a maximum of six months' imprisonment, twelve strokes, or a fine or five pounds.

52. Lord Hailey, *Native Administration in the British African Territories*, 5 Vols. (London: 1951), Part III, p. 167.

53. *Ibid.*, p. 165.

Index

Aba, 65, 86, 109, 112, 113, 117-20, 121, 126, 130, 139

Aba Division, 11, 89, 90, 92, 120, 136, 148

Abak District, 123-24, 125, 126, 130, 132, 136, 137

Abakaliki Division, 20

Abam, 29

Abeskuta, 37

Aboh, 35

Accra, 41

Achara, 151

Adams, F. B., 81

Afikpo, 49

Afikpo Division, 11, 20, 22, 137

Agatu Division, 11

Age sets, 16, 24, 25

Ahoada Division, 11, 20, 122, 137, 148

Ajasa, Sir Kitayi, 138

Akassa, 44

Akitoye (King of Lagos), 35

Akpa, 28, 29

Akpan Obo, Chief, 123

Akpan Udo Lekpo, Chief, 103

Akpan Umo, Chief, 124, 125

Akulechula, 131 ·

Akwette, 48

Alexander, C. W., 82, 84, 120, 144, 156

Aloyi, 137

Amachree (King of New Calabar), 53

Amanyanabo, 12, 13

Amery, Leopold (Colonial Secretary), 85

Anang, 14-15

Andoni-Ibeno, 14, 15

Army units: In Calabar, 123, 124-25; in Eastern areas, 136, 140; in Opobo, 127-28; in Owerri, 120

Aro people, 13, 14, 28, 29, 32-33, 45, 47

Aro-Chukwu, 20, 28, 48, 129

Aro Expedition, 24, 48-49

Asa Court Area, 90, 117, 120
Asaba, 42, 49
Ashanti, 47, 48
Asiga, 46
Assessment reports, 85-94
Awgu, 104
Awka, 72
Ayaba Court Area, 89, 112
Azumini Court Area, 120

Badagry, 37
Baikie, William, 36, 38
Baro, 66
Bathurst, 3
Beecroft, John, 35
Bende, 11, 15, 45, 49
Bende Division, 20, 89, 92, 93, 104, 106, 109-12, 115, 137
Benin Kingdom, 24, 44, 46, 52, 53
Benin Province, 10, 20
Benin River, 10, 39, 43
Blackall, Henry, 137, 138
Bonny, 10, 12, 32, 34, 35, 38, 47, 52, 53, 104
Bonny River, 10, 14
Borgu, 52
Boyle, A. G., 77
Brass, 12, 32, 39, 44
Brass River, 10
British expansion, 35-37, 39-40, 41-42, 43-49
Brohemie, 43
Browning, Lt., 124
Buchanan-Smith, Capt. W., 144, 157, 158

Calabar Province, 10, 11, 14, 20, 71, 72, 77, 89, 91, 96, 99, 100, 101, 113, 117, 122, 129, 135, 136, 138, 139, 148-49, 150, 151, 154
Cameron, Sir Donald, 7, 141, 146-48, 154, 155, 158
Chamberlain, Joseph (Colonial Secretary), 1, 47
Chanomi (Gov. of Itsekiri), 39
Church Missionary Society, 37
Church of Scotland, 37

Clapperton, 33
Clifford, Sir Hugh, 72, 73, 75-80, 96, 155, 158-59
Cochrane, K. A. B., 87, 91, 159
Collective Punishment Ordinance, 135
Compagnie Française de l' Afrique Équatoriale, 40
Compagnie du Sénégal et de la Côte Occidental d'Afrique, 40
Commission of Inquiry (First), 124, 137-38
Commission of Inquiry (Second), 118, 128, 130, 138-43
Congress of Berlin, 40
Cook, Capt. John, 106-107, 139
Creek Town, 15
Cross River, 10, 14, 15, 46, 48, 49, 52, 55
Crowther, Rev. Samuel, 38
Customs duties, 99-100

Dancing Women's Movement, 104, 105, 106
Degema, 47, 53, 87, 88, 104
Diala, 25
Diokpa, 23
Draft Tax Ordinance, 1926, 81-82, 83

Eastern Ibibio, 14
Efik, 14, 15-16, 149
Egerton, Sir Walter, 49, 59, 60, 67, 159
Eke-Apara, 118
Eket, 14, 15
Ekoi area, 94
Ekuri, 46
Elele District, 87, 93
Emeruwa, Mark, 108-109, 111, 139, 141
Enugu, 11, 110
Enyong, 14, 15
Equipment Treaty, 34
Essene Court Area, 115, 117
Ete Ekpuk, 16
Ete Idung, 16
Ete Otung, 16

Etuboms, 15, 149, 150
Extended family, 12, 16, 22
Eze Aro, 28
Ezza subtribe, 95
Ezzi subtribe, 95, 105

Falk, E. M., 91, 117, 126, 140, 159
Fines for disturbances, 136
Freetown, 3
Findley, G. H., 159-60
Firth, O. W., 93, 160
Floyer, Cadet R. H., 115, 126, 140
Forcados River, 10, 151
Ford, E. T. P., 123-24
French expansion, 2, 42
Futa Jallon, 10

Galway, H. L., 54, 63
German expansion, 41
Gray, William, 137, 138
Green, M. M., 24, 25
Grier, S. M., 72-73, 77-78, 80, 84, 88, 133, 160

Hailey, Lord, 154
Harcourt, Lord (Colonial Secretary), 75
Hargrove, Reginald, 64
Hewitt, Consul, 41
High Court of the Native Council of Old Calabar, 53
Hill, Capt. J. N., 106, 110-12, 127, 128, 130
House Rule Proclamations of 1899 and 1901, 54
House system, 13, 14, 15-16, 32, 35, 38, 54
Hunt, W. E., 86, 138, 160
Hunter, Dr., 118-19

Ibadan, 37
Ibibio, 11, 13-20, 45, 54
Ibibio languages, 12, 14
Ibo, 20-30, 42, 45, 46, 47, 48-49, 52, 54, 81, 87
Ibo languages, 12, 21, 24
Ido, 49
Ijaw, 12-14, 15, 32, 33, 81

Ika Court Area, 123
Ikonnia, 108
Ikot-Ekpene Division, 14, 64, 86, 105, 109, 117, 139
Ikot-Obio-Itong, 115, 126
Ikpa clan, 115
Imo River, 14
Ingles, F. H., 119, 160
Intelligence Reports, 145-46, 148-49
Isu District, 93
Isuachi clan, 151
Itsekiri, 39, 43
Itu, 14, 48, 86, 105, 129

Jackson, John, 89, 90, 117-18
Jaja (King of Opobo), 38, 41
James, Capt. H. P., 123, 124-25
Jebba, 52
Jekris, 90
Jenkins, J. F., 89, 90
Johnston, Sir Harry H., 41, 52

Kingdon, Donald, 84, 86, 138
Kosoko (King of Lagos), 35
Kwa Ibo River, 10, 41, 46
Kwa language group, 21

Lagos, 3, 35, 36, 39, 61, 139, 155
Lagos Colony and Protectorate, 49, 51, 60
Laird, MacGregor, 35, 36
Land ownership, 26-27
Lander, John, 33
Lander, Richard, 33
Lawrence, C. T., 139, 144-45
Leeming, Capt. A., 88
Legislative Council on Riots, 142
Liverpool, 35
Localized patrilineage, 22-23
Lokoja, 35, 42
Long Juju, 13, 28, 29, 47, 49
Lugard, Lord Frederick, 3, 7, 29, 45, 50, 62, 65-73, 75-77, 80, 96, 153, 160-61

MacDonald, Sir Claude, 43-45, 51-53, 161

Markets, 27-28
Mark Pepple Jaja, 125, 130, 131
Mayne, C. T., 87, 92
Mbala, 151
Mbwpongo, 107
Meek, C. K., 145
Menendez, Justice M., 59
Men's role in disturbances, 130-31, 133
Mikiri, 25, 101
Minna, 66
Missionaries, 21, 35-38
Montanaro, Lt.-Col., 43-49, 55
Moor, Sir Ralph, 3, 29, 43-49, 53, 54-56, 67, 161-62
Moore, Eric Olowolu, 138
Moorhouse, Sir Harry, 80, 162
Muris, 150

Nana (Gov. of Itsekiri), 39, 43, 45
National Africa Co., 40
Native Authorities, 148-49, 149-50, 151
Native Authority Ordinance, 1916, 70-71
Native Authority Ordinance, 1933, 153
Native Court Clerks, 6, 57, 58, 64, 69-70
Native court messengers, 70
Native courts: under Cameron, 150-51, 153; under Egerton, 61-62; under Lugard, 68-72; under MacDonald, 52-53; under Moor, 59-60
Native Courts Ordinance, 1914, 68-70, 72
Native Courts Ordinance, 1933, 153
Native Courts Proclamation, 1900, 56-57, 68
Native Courts Proclamation, 1901, 57-58, 65, 68
Native Courts Proclamation, 1906, 61-62, 65, 68
Native Revenue Ordinance, 1917, 81, 83, 84
Native Treasuries, 153-54
Naval patrols, 36, 39, 42, 43-44

Ndi ichie, 24
Ndi igbo, 21
Ndi olu, 21
Ndumani, 64
Nembe, 44, 53
New Calabar, 12, 32, 53
New Calabar River, 10
Ngor, 49, 121, 136
Nguru, 121, 136
Ngwa clan, 112, 117
Niger Coast Protectorates, 43, 52, 60
Niger River, 9, 10, 33, 36, 37, 38, 42
Nigerian Council, 67
Nigerian unification, 66-67
Nikki, 42
Norio-Ovoro, 49
Nsukka, 86, 145
Ntoes, 150
Nun River, 10
Nupe, 36, 42
Nwannedie, 108
Nwanyeruwa, 108-109, 111, 112, 155
Nwugo, 108

Obinkita, 28
Obohia Court Area, 120, 136
Obowo, 122, 131
Obuzza, 137
Ochi District, 93
Ofo, 23
Ogoja Province, 10, 20, 71, 72, 77, 95, 105, 137
Oguta, 48, 49, 121, 137
Oha ndi nyiom, 132
Ohu, 25-26
Oil Rivers Protectorate, 2, 41, 43-44, 51
Ojim, 108
Oke Nache, 28
Okigwi District, 11, 86, 87, 91, 94, 104, 108, 131
Okikra, 12, 32, 52, 53
Oko-Jumbo, 38
Okopedi, 129
Okoyong, 28
Okpala Court Area, 22, 121

Okugo, Chief, 107-10, 111, 112, 114, 139, 141
Old Calabar, 13, 15, 20, 32, 36, 55
Oloko, 28, 89, 107-15, 128, 130, 155
Olokwo, 121
Omuma Court Area, 120
Onitsha Ibo, 21
Onitsha Province, 10, 11, 20, 71, 72, 77, 94, 95
Onitsha Town, 35, 49
Opara, 23
Opobo Division, 14, 52, 115, 126
Opobo Town, 38, 39, 41, 46, 47, 115, 117, 126, 127, 130, 132, 136, 137, 139, 140
Orlu Division, 11
Oron tribe, 15
Osborne, Chief Justice, 69
Osborne, Ronald, 138, 139
Osu, 25, 26
Owerri Division, 11, 135, 136, 138, 139, 145
Owerri Ibo, 21
Owerri Province, 10, 11, 65, 71, 72, 77, 80, 86, 87, 89, 99, 100, 101, 102, 104, 106, 112, 113, 117, 122, 126, 148, 150-51, 153, 154
Owerri Town, 49, 64, 109, 112, 121-22, 139
Owerrinta Court Area, 117, 121, 131, 136
Ozo, 101

Palmer, H. Richmond, 76, 82, 84, 162
Palm oil trade, 11, 14, 28, 34-35, 90, 98-99, 137, 152
Passfield, Lord (Col. Secretary), 141, 142-43, 147
Paul, Graham, 138, 139, 140-43
Peace Preservation Ordinance, 120, 135, 137
Phillips, J. B., 44
Police force: at Aba, 118, 119-20; at Abak, 123; at Calabar, 122; at Opobo, 127; at Owerri, 117, 120
Political organization (traditional): Aro, 28-29

Efik, 15-16
Eket, 15
Ibibio, 15-18, 86, 145-46
Ibo, 20-25, 29, 63, 86, 145-46
Ijaw, 12-13
Population density, 11, 14-15
Port Harcourt, 114, 117, 121, 126
Portuguese, 31, 34
Protectorate government organization: under Cameron, 148-55; under Clifford, 78-80; under Egerton, 59-62; under Lugard, 65-73, 75-77; under MacDonald, 52-53; under Moor, 55-59; under Thomson, 85-88, 144-46
Punitive expeditions, 136-37

Roads and Rivers Ordinance, 84
Royal Niger Co., 40-42, 45, 46, 50, 51, 54
Ruxton, Maj. U. F., 81, 82-83, 93, 162

Sasse, R. H. J., 81
Second Hundred Years War, 31
Select Committee of 1865, 36, 39
Slavery, 13, 25-26, 32
Slave trade, 12, 15, 25, 29, 31-34
Sobo, 90
Southern Nigeria Legislative Council, 67
Southern Nigerian Protectorate, 49, 54, 60-61, 67
Special Commissioner Courts, 58
Spirit movement, 104-105
Stockley, G. E., 88
Supreme Court, 58, 61, 62, 69

Talbot, P. Amaury, 81
Taubman, George Goldie (Sir George Goldie), 40-45
Taylor, Rev. J. C., 38
Tax assessment, 6-7, 85-84
Tax collection methods, 94-96, 143, 152
Tax reduction, 152-53
Taxation:
  Grier's warnings, 77-78
  Lugard's ideas, 75-77

Ruxton's proposals, 82-83
Thomson's taxing system, 83-95
Tomlinson's report, 78-80
Thomas, Northcote, 67
Thomson, Sir Graeme, 72, 75, 80, 83, 85, 135, 137, 140, 141, 142-44, 155, 162
Title Societies (Ibibio): Ebre, 17, 100-101, 102; Ekong, 17; Ekpe, 17, 105; Ekpo, 17; Idiong, 17, 105
Title Societies (Ibo): 23-24; Eyoro, 101; Ogbo, 102, 131
Tomlinson, G. J. F., 73, 75-80, 82, 84, 162-63
Traders: Aro, 29, 32-33, 47; British, 21, 31-37, 40-42; French, 39-40; Ibibio, 14, 34; Ibo, 27-28; Ijaw, 12-14, 32-33; Portuguese, 34; Spanish, 34

Udoko Division, 11
Ukam Court Area, 115, 126
Umuahia, 87, 111-12, 115
Umuaturu Court Area, 122, 132, 136
Umuchieze, 151
Umunna, 22
Umuosu, 107
Union Ibo, 20
United Africa Co., 40
Unwana, 48

Utu-Etim-Ekpo, 123, 124, 125, 132, 137
Uyo Division, 14, 123

Warrant Chiefs, 6, 55, 62-64, 70, 75, 84-85, 86, 88, 102, 105, 106, 123, 144-45, 149
Warri Province, 11, 20, 39, 52, 72, 77, 86, 90, 93, 152
Weir, A. L., 106, 122
Whitman, A. R., 87, 115, 125, 126-28, 140
Women's disturbances: 7, 20, 88, 89, 103-106, 115, 130-33; at Aba, 117-20; at Abak, 123-24; at Aro Chukwu, 129; at Okigwi, 122; at Okopedi, 129; at Oloko, 108-13; at Opobo Town, 127-29; at Owerri Town, 121; at Ukam, 126; at Utu-Etim-Ekpo, 124-25
Women's role: in Ibibio marriage, 17; in Ibo marriage, 22, 23, 26; in land ownership, 26-27, 100; in political decisions, 22, 25; in secret societies, 17-18, 23; in trade, 18, 25, 27-28, 98, 100

Yam production, 11, 14, 27
Yorubaland, 36, 37